The author and her mother at a beach in Maine, circa 1975.
Credit: Edward Robillard; source: Amy E. Robillard

# We Find Ourselves in Other People's Stories

*We Find Ourselves in Other People's Stories: On Narrative Collapse and a Lifetime Search for Story* is a collection of five essays that dissolves the boundary between personal writing and academic writing, a long-standing binary construct in the discipline of composition and writing studies, in order to examine the rhetorical effects of narrative collapse on the stories we tell about ourselves and others. Taken together, the essays theorize the relationships between language and violence, between narrative and dementia, between genre and certainty, and between writing and life.

**Amy E. Robillard** is Professor of English at Illinois State University, USA. She is editor, with Ron Fortune, of *Authorship Contested: Cultural Challenges to the Authentic, Autonomous Author,* and her work has appeared in a number of professional journals. Her personal essays have appeared on *The Rumpus* and on *Full Grown People.*

# We Find Ourselves in Other People's Stories

## On Narrative Collapse and a Lifetime Search for Story

Amy E. Robillard

Routledge
Taylor & Francis Group

LONDON AND NEW YORK

First published 2019 by Routledge

2 Park Square, Milton Park, Abingdon, Oxon, OX14 4RN

605 Third Avenue, New York, NY 10017

*Routledge is an imprint of the Taylor & Francis Group, an informa business*

First issued in paperback 2020

*Library of Congress Cataloging-in-Publication Data*
A catalog record for this title has been requested

ISBN: 978-1-138-39328-8 (hbk)
ISBN: 978-0-367-78811-7 (pbk)

Typeset in Sabon
by codeMantra

In the history of the world, a whole story has never been told.
—Meghan Daum, *The Unspeakable*


Aren't we all woven through with stories? Isn't that how we think of our lives, how we survive them? Now, when someone hurts me, I remember that they are only living the terms of their own fictions—sometimes desperately—so their selves don't unravel.
—Lidia Yuknavitch, "Woven"

# Contents

# Preface

My mother told me that when I was born I was taken from her, rushed to a hospital in Hartford, Connecticut, that was equipped to care for my racing heart in ways Holyoke Hospital in Massachusetts wasn't. I was a big baby—ten pounds, fourteen ounces—and the doctor had to break my shoulder to get me out. I was born broken and overexcited and had to be on digitalis for the first year of my life. I am not a mother, but it isn't hard for me to imagine how hard it must've been for my mother to have me taken away right after birth. When I asked her if I was all alone, she said my father went to visit me. Visit me? How long was I there, I wonder now. I sometimes think of this early separation as a possible reason for the distance between Ma and me. We never had the chance to bond early on. No skin-on-skin contact. Instead I imagine anxiety and fear and maybe even panic. Her baby was being taken from her and there was nothing she could do.

We cannot write our beginnings or our endings; others must do that for us. They are our life stories, but we cannot tell them. We cannot set the terms of their narration. We can know what our entry into this world was like only by way of others' accounts. And while we can perhaps write up until the end of our lives, we can never know how it will go. We can't know what it's like for the people we leave behind. They must, if they're so inclined, write their own accounts.

I am only one of the people my mother left behind, and I write these accounts not to claim that they are the right or true versions but to try to come to terms with a fraught relationship in the only way I know how: by writing, by theorizing, by bringing into our relationship some of the voices, ideas, and concepts that populate my inner life. My mother and her story, for all of their problems, made me and my story possible. I owe her my life and I owe her my story. I always used to say that she was never meant to be a mother; in saying this I was also implying, for the careful listener, that I was never really supposed to be here. But then, who among us is?

My aim, too, is to reveal something about the way narrative works in our lives, the work it does to hold us together, the work it does to keep us apart. Though we talk rather unproblematically about the story of our lives, there is always more than one, but never at one time. Narratives replace one another. Narratives disrupt one another. Narratives trouble one another. And narratives collapse. And just as a building collapse affects the structures surrounding it, so too does a narrative collapse affect the structures surrounding it.

*

Here, then, are my explicit goals in composing these connected essays about narrative, illness, dementia, abortion, abuse, neglect, secrets, and mostly, loss. Taken together, these essays

1   Dissolve the boundary between personal writing and academic writing in order to examine the rhetorical effects of narrative collapse on the stories we tell about ourselves and others.
2   Relax the tiresome truisms about the boundary between the academic and the personal, the simplicity of narrative, and the insignificance of writing about the self that have maintained a stronghold on composition and writing studies for decades.
3   Theorize narratives that collapse as those that can no longer be supported by cultural, social, and political conditions, whose themes cannot be supported by what is outside itself. Narratives that cannot be so supported cave in on themselves, taking others with them.
4   Distinguish between the narrative construction to which we refer during most of our life and the narrative preservation we turn to at the end of life when memory begins to fail us.
5   Point to the ways we can draw on narrative resources—cultural stories from which we assemble our own stories—without ever actually telling the story we want to tell. In other words, these essays demonstrate the ways we can tell our stories slant forever—either by issuing cautions as my mother did or by simply engaging in scholarship and teaching, as so many of us do.
6   Theorize the relationship between stories told slant and cautionary tales.
7   Evidence the ways in which the dominant cultural narratives about, for example, abortion—women either regret or do not regret their decisions—are framed obscure narratives that are less dramatic but perhaps far more important. For instance, that an abortion made this scholar's teaching and writing life possible is a narrative we hear far too seldom.
8   Reflect on the teaching of the personal essay and on representations of illness.

My suspicion, and my hope, is that as you read these essays, you will find yourself reflecting on the ways you have been telling your own stories slant and perhaps vow to straighten out one or two. If not for others, certainly not for the field, but for your own understanding of why you do what you do.

# Acknowledgments

For their support of this project and for their work that pushes boundaries, I thank Joseph Harris, Richard E. Miller, and Beth Boquet. At Routledge, I am grateful to Hannah Shakespeare and Jennifer Abbott, who helped shepherd this book to completion. To Hillary Reale, my oldest and dearest friend, thank you for reading versions of this and always believing in the value of this work. Thanks, too, to Ron Fortune and Sarah Hochstetler for your encouragement, support, and your precious time as readers throughout this process; your friendship makes me a better writer. Thank you, Bill White, for so many things, but mostly for helping me see and believe differently. I'm so grateful to my aunt Judy Crump for her willingness to share both my mother's story and her own story with me. To my husband, Steve Field, thank you for your faithful support and enduring enthusiasm as I wrote the many revisions of this book. I'm so grateful for everything you give me. And to Wrigley and Essay, thank you for keeping me company through so much of the writing of this book. Your soft snores and tail flaps keep me going.

# 1 Learning to Keep My Distance

> You freeze up in childhood, you go numb, because you cannot change
> your circumstances and to recognize, name, and feel the emotions and
> their cruel causes would be unbearable, and so you wait.
> —Rebecca Solnit, *The Faraway Nearby*

My father was a photographer, dedicated to the art of framing a scene,
a moment, a memory. Dedicated to composition, lighting, mood, to
capturing what does not stay.

My father died when I was four years old, and though I carry with me
a memory of finding him lying blue on the basement floor, my brother
Guy, three years older than me, carries with him the same memory of
*himself* finding our father. "I remember going down those old wooden
stairs," he tells me. "I remember it as if I did it. I don't know if somebody
else put it in my head to make me think I remember it. Maybe we all came
home at once and went down there." My oldest sister Sue remembers
coming home from school to find a fire truck, ambulance, and police car
turning down our street. Panic set in as she saw them stop in front of
our house. Sue remembers seeing him lying there on the cement floor, a
puddle by his legs, his skin gray as the paramedics performed CPR. Tim,
who turned fourteen the day before our father died, recalls only that
he had dragged Dad through the store a couple days earlier because he
wanted a race car set. "I made Dad take me up to Two Guys. I was being
a little brat bastard and he's limping through the store. Come to find out
it was a clot. A coronary occlusion that went to his heart. A few days
later Don Burgess comes up the stairs holding a huge package. 'Look
what I found for you, Tim.' Talk about feeling low."

When we were young and our father was still alive, he was in the
hospital a lot. He had a number of heart attacks before the fatal one at
age fifty. I remember picking him up from the hospital and hiding behind
the passenger seat on the floor of the car and him searching for me.
"Where's Amy?" he'd ask, with exaggerated bewilderment. I'd jump up
then, surprising him, and he'd laugh, and we'd go to The Pancake House
down the street from the hospital.

2 Learning to Keep My Distance

Guy tells me, "I very vaguely remember him taking us to the park and flying a kite on Sunday after catechism. We didn't even know him. I know he smoked a lot. I remember him smoking Pall Malls. It's weird that Timmy and Susie remember so much."

Guy also remembers the time he and Margie were home alone and Dad went to the store to get cigarettes but never came home. "Both of us kneeling on the couch, looking out the window saying, 'I wonder where he is.' I think he ended up going to the hospital. Maybe Ma was in the hospital with you or something. But I'll never forget that day. No, that's right. Ma called the hospital. He had checked himself in."

The way I heard this story told was that he told Guy and Margie he was going out for cigarettes, but he knew he had to go to the hospital. He knew he was about to have another heart attack, but he didn't want Ma to know because she would get upset with him and yell and scream. So he just left. When Ma came home from wherever she had been, she called Dad's friends looking for him. Like she was looking for a child. Finally Ed Jubinville told her he knew where Dad was, but she had to promise not to yell at him when she talked to him. She promised. But she yelled at him anyway.

Ma hated for anybody to be sick. She felt like they were abandoning her on purpose. She was angry when he finally died and left her with five kids to raise by herself.

My father was, by all accounts, a kind man. He smoked too much, sure, but he was loving and generous, creative and optimistic, funny and fun-loving. Aside from what we inherited from him physically, the only things my siblings and I share from our father are the stories of how we lost him. The three oldest share more than that, surely. But Guy and me, we're left with very little. The only things about which we can say, "No, it happened this way" or "No, I remember it like this" are the stories about how he died and how he snuck away to be sick in private.

Ma never told us much about him. When I would ask her questions about him, she'd respond by telling me she didn't know or she didn't remember, or she would try to distract me by telling me to look at the cat or asking me if I didn't have anything better to do.

Dad died in December 1976. Five months later, in May 1977, my mother's firstborn, my half-sister Pam, died of kidney failure brought on by pancreatitis at the age of twenty-two. I don't have very many memories of Pam. I have more memories of Pam's two daughters, Lee Ann and Kelly, who were very close in age to me. Pam had become pregnant at the age of fifteen with Lee Ann, and fifteen months after Lee Ann was born, she gave birth to Kelly. Pam was pregnant with Kelly at the same time Ma was pregnant with me. We three played together when we were young.

I like to believe that, as her youngest child, I was my mother's comfort during this incredibly difficult time. That she was depressed should go without saying. I think now about the serpentine nature of the processes I've gone through grieving losses while surrounded by a supportive husband and friends, a therapist I trust deeply and completely, all while living in a culture far more educated about just how crucial grieving is to a healthy life, and I want to travel through time to hug my young mother, about the age I am now as I write. If she talked about her grief, it was minimal. If she processed it at all, it was likely very briefly with friends who probably couldn't understand and, with the best of intentions, encouraged her to move on for the kids' sake. Sue remembers Ma telling her, not days after Dad died, not to cry. "I think she just didn't know what else to say to me, didn't know how to show compassion maybe?"

It really is no wonder, then, that she wasn't a good mother. I mean, how could she be?

*

Most of us don't have very many memories before the age of three or four. The abuse surely began after my father died. Thus, nearly the entirety of my childhood memories includes the abuse I suffered at the hands of my older sister, Margie, five years older than me. She would have been nine when our father died.

I remember it was a Sunday night, and Timmy was supposed to be babysitting me, but I don't know where he was. Guy was upstairs, Susie was out, and Margie was beating me. She was chasing me around the kitchen table, punching me when she caught me, and I was screaming for someone to help. She wanted me to shut the fuck up. I screamed louder. She ran into the living room and grabbed Ma's chair, the one she always sat in when she wasn't sleeping on the couch. She lifted it over her head and made her way toward me. She was going to hit me with the chair! I ran out the back door screaming. She opened the door and dragged me back in, squeezing bruises into my arm. "You're fucking dead." My heart was pounding. I had nowhere to go. I kept screaming for my mommy. She punched me in the nose. It started bleeding. She seemed satisfied to have drawn blood. I went to the couch to sit and cry, the snot mixing with the blood, all of it dripping onto my shirt and onto my bare knees. I tried to convince myself that if I just sat here long enough and let Ma see what she'd let happen to me, she would do something. She would make it stop.

Instead, when she saw me, she told me to stay away from Margie. "Mind your own business and she'll leave you alone."

Susie and Margie shared the room next to mine, and the house was configured so that to get to their room, they had to go through mine—just a few steps, but enough to make me feel like I could never really shut the door or shut them out. My door was always open. Actually, all three bedrooms upstairs were connected. Inside Susie and Margie's room was a door that led to Guy and Timmy's room, but it wouldn't have made much sense for the girls to walk all the way through the boys' room to get to theirs, not when it was so much easier to walk through mine.

Bedtime. Margie walked through to her room. "You little shit. You're dead."

Middle of the night. Margie walked back through to the one bathroom in the house. "Little fucker. Fat shit."

Back to her room. "Skank."

Morning. "You're dead, you little shit."

And so it went. Always. I wonder now if her insults became so habitual as she walked those couple steps through my room that she said them even when I wasn't there.

She was always hitting me for no reason, punching my arm or my stomach, and I'd cry out for my mother, and my mother would tell me to stay away from her, to go do something else. She threatened to kill me always, telling me that as soon as Ma left, I was dead. I feared for my life before I could walk to school alone. She beat me in front of her own friends, and when they begged her to stop, she simply didn't hear them.

She instilled in me a white-hot self-hatred that has taken years to dissolve.

I understand now that Margie did what she did to me out of fear and insecurity, out of a desperate need for discipline and care. I understand that she had the same mother I had, the same mother who was terribly depressed by two suffocating losses, either one of which would have been more than enough to turn what might have been a good mother into a bad mother. My sister's abuse shaped me into a person deathly afraid of conflict, convinced of her own insignificance, fatness, ugliness, and stupidity, persuaded that she was completely on her own in this world because nobody would help her when she needed it most. Ma told me to stay away from her, so I tried. I was a kid. I believed that if I did what my mother told me to do, I might be okay. I turned to reading instead. I read and read and read. Reading helped me keep my distance.

The librarian at the Willimansett branch library loved me. She encouraged me to read above my grade level, and she put aside new books she knew I'd enjoy. I'd read all the V.C. Andrews books by the eighth grade and was particularly haunted by *My Sweet Audrina*. How could the parents convince Audrina that it was her *sister* who'd been raped in the woods and that she was the second Audrina? Imagine how much her parents had to love her to do such a thing. My librarian lived over on Pickering Street near Julie Veremey's house. Julie and I would ride our bikes down her gravelly street, and I would fantasize about her seeing me and inviting me in to pore over her bookshelves and take whatever I wanted.

I read to escape my family life. I read to escape Ma and Margie and Guy and Timmy and Susie. Sometimes Mindy, our cat, would sleep on my bed as I lay in it and read, but mostly I was alone and that's the way I liked it. Leave me alone. When I was deep in a book, I was in another place, a place where parents loved their children and sat with them at the breakfast table, a place where siblings gave each other cute nicknames like Fudgie or Tootsie or Beezus and nobody got beaten for it. In my books, parents told kids to be kind to their siblings, and if they weren't, they'd be grounded. If I'm completely honest, I'll admit that to this very day, I'm still taken aback by true stories of siblings who love one another or, more to the point, by true stories of siblings who don't recall with deep resentment their childhoods together.

At the end of fifth grade, Mrs. Lefebvre filled out a reading certificate for every kid in the class, writing the number of books each kid had read during the school year. When she called me up to her desk to receive my certificate, she told me that she'd had to estimate because every time she looked up at me, I was reading a different book. She gave me my certificate and told me she was proud of me, that I should be proud of myself. In the blank space reserved for the number, Mrs. Lefebvre had written 80. My teacher was proud of me.

*

Margie and I played "the dying game" a lot. This consisted of Margie lying on the floor and me jumping on top of her as hard as I could until she couldn't take it anymore and she'd declare herself dead. I'd stop jumping then. I was never on the bottom in this game, only Margie. It was as though only in play could I become the aggressor. Only when it was make believe. When it was for real, I never stood a chance.

*

When I was seven years old, Ma met a man she wanted to marry, and when she told me, I remember asking her if this meant I would have a new daddy. Warren had a wooden leg, two grown children, and three grandchildren, the oldest, Nina, who was my age. Warren moved in and he seemed to like Sue and Tim the best. I know he didn't like me much because I was, as he said, spoiled rotten, and I ate too much candy, and my mother gave me everything I ever asked for. He didn't like the way Guy and Margie talked to Ma. In the beginning Ma would make me kiss him goodnight before bed. This strikes me now as sweet, an effort, anyway. At the time, though, I hated it. His cheek always smelled like smoke and was rough from stubble. He didn't seem to like it much more than I did.

My memories of Warren and Ma together mostly have to do with the Sunday drives the three of us would take through the towns of western

Massachusetts. We'd pass what I used to think was the pie maker but was actually some kind of water treatment plant on the way to Atkin's Farms in Hadley, where we'd buy apples and cider donuts and sometimes cider. I could always count on Ma to get carsick on these Sunday drives, and that usually meant that we'd stop for something to eat to soothe her nausea. An ice cream at Friendly's usually did the trick. My favorite was chocolate with chocolate sprinkles. Astonishingly, Ma would complain when she asked for a small cone and they gave her too much ice cream. She'd always say that she'd hate to see the large.

I'm not sure when Ma began cheating on Warren or how I found out about it. It just seems now that I always knew about Hank. And later Merrill. I don't remember the day I met Hank, but I do remember him driving me back to college more than once after semester breaks. He had a clothing rod in the back of his car that he was very eager for me to use to hang my clothes on for the ride back to Worcester. I'd met Hank many times before this, and I think I was the only one of us kids who did.

As I grew up, Ma told me in so many different ways that men were bad news. She'd tell me directly to stay away from men. We'd be watching television together, and she would never fail to comment on the male characters who did things wrong, saying, "What a goddamn idiot." We'd be in the mall together and she'd see a man walking our way and she'd say, too loudly, "Jesus Christ, he's ugly." She'd say, when I'd complain about something Warren had done, "If he had a brain, he'd be dangerous." Men were no good, stupid, idiotic, and generally ugly.

I remember one day when I borrowed Guy's van to drive myself back to Syracuse, where I was working on my PhD. It was a beat-up old thing, but it would get me where I needed to go, so I didn't care. The passenger door was held on by a combination of bungee cords, canvas straps, and duct tape. When Ma saw the door as I was leaving to get on the road, she said, "Good. That way no man can jump in and get you."

But. They were also necessary. "Marry a rich man," I heard countless times as I grew up. "Make sure you marry a doctor." Susie used to tell me about how Ma would warn her not to go behind the bushes with boys. I never heard that one, but I was told more directly not to get pregnant before I got married because she sure as shit wasn't going to take care of any babies. Over and over again, I learned that I needed to marry a rich man who wouldn't get me pregnant before he married me.

It wasn't hard to attribute this to Pam. Pam had gotten pregnant when she was just fifteen, and her boyfriend Don got her pregnant again nearly immediately after Lee Ann was born. Sue tells me that Ma forced them to get married. Two weeks after Pam gave birth to Kelly, she was in the hospital with failing kidneys. She was diagnosed with pancreatitis. If this had happened to her while she'd been pregnant, they both probably would've died.

I've always known that Pam died when she was twenty-two. Kidney failure brought on by pancreatitis, I told anyone who asked. I memorized this fact, but I never really knew what it meant. I never really knew what my mother went through watching her daughter die slowly and painfully.

She suffered for five years.

About two years in, the doctors gathered with my mother and Don to get a sense of how they felt about pulling the plug. These are the words my mother used.

"Pulling the plug? Wouldn't that imply that she was plugged into a respirator?"
"It's just a saying."

Ma was in favor of pulling the plug, but Don was not. "So he decided to let her suffer for a few more years," Ma tells me. "I wouldn't let a dog suffer the way she suffered. It was disgusting."

Don was the husband. It was his decision to make.

Where were the babies during all this, I ask. With Don's mother. Did Pam ever get to see them? Sure, Don would bring them in when he could. She didn't get to leave the hospital very often because of the dialysis, but on the days that she could, he'd run through the hospital pushing that wheelchair so fast he nearly knocked other patients over. He was so happy to get her out of there.

Men were trouble not just because they could jump into the passenger door of the beat-up old van you were driving but because they could keep you alive and suffering when all you wanted to do was let go.

*

Ma used to tell us that we needed to have children so they could take care of us when we got older. She told us to have more than one because if you had only one and something happened to that child, you'd never recover.

She told us to be careful what we wished for because we just might get it. She told us to behave when we left the house. She told us to go chase ourselves, to go to someone else's house, to leave her alone. She told us to quiet down because, for Christ's sake, she couldn't hear herself think.

She never told us what she was thinking about.

*

School was my safe place, the only place where I was noticed for anything good. At home I was a brat or I was spoiled or I was a picky eater or I was a little shit or I was dead as soon as Ma left the house. But at school I was smart. I was a good student, obedient, eager to please, and a quick study. I was the fastest kid in school when it came to math races, and I won all the spelling bees until Christopher Goff showed up in sixth grade. In fourth grade Mr. Cunningham would give the spelling bee winner a dollar as a prize. I used it to buy candy. In sixth grade Mr. Lysek gave huge Disney stickers he'd buy on his annual trip down to Florida. I stuck my Donald Duck sticker on my bedroom door. Margie promptly wrote a swear word on it on her way into her room.

I was always afraid, always insecure, always sure that everybody hated me. Other kids asked my friends why I never smiled. I thought about death all the time—my own, Margie's. I was desperate for attention at school, so I did everything I could to make sure my teachers noticed me. When in fourth grade Mr. Cunningham told me that the other fourth-grade teacher, Mr. Foley, remembered my dad from his wedding, I was overcome with longing for that memory. Mr. Foley even had some video of my dad somewhere in his basement. "He was a good man," Mr. Cunningham told me.

I met Hillary when she was the new girl in class in the fifth grade. She was tall and thin and had long brown hair. She lived on Narragansett Boulevard, which was about ten blocks away from our house on Ferry Street. We'd walk to and from one another's houses all the time, and we'd always meet each other halfway. If she was coming to my house, I'd meet her halfway at the corner of Norman and Chicopee Streets, and we'd walk back together. When I'd leave her house to walk home at night, she'd walk me halfway, and then we'd each walk the rest of the way home alone. I would carefully consider which of the two routes— the busier Chicopee Street route or the quieter Norman/Skeele Street route—was less likely to harbor murderers, and I'd take that one. The next time I'd choose the other route, just to throw them off. I always had the sense I was being watched.

We played Scrabble and Trivial Pursuit and made prank phone calls to the boys we liked and ate Stella D'oro breakfast treats and potato chips and straightened our naturally curly hair and experimented with makeup.

As an adult I read that traumatized people calculate life's chances differently. As a kid I knew this in my bones. I knew I wanted to be a writer, but I also knew I had to hurry because I likely wouldn't make it much past twenty-seven. I knew I'd die early not because I was sick or because I expected to be in some kind of horrible accident but because I knew I just wasn't meant to live a long life. My sister's constant beating me down took its toll on my ability to imagine a future. I was fat, ugly, stupid, worthless, and a pain in the ass. I was told this at least ten times a day. I was told this while I was sleeping. I was never meant to live past twenty-seven because I'd probably kill myself before then.

Hillary understood. She, too, knew she wouldn't live to be very old. She lived with her mom and her sister Hope, who was just a year older than Hillary. They lived in a tiny apartment above their firefighter landlord. The way the apartment was configured, you could walk up the front stairs to the apartment and take a left to Hillary and Hope's room without going through the rest of the apartment. If you took a right, you'd open the door into the kitchen, living room, bathroom, and Hillary's mom's room. But if you took that immediate left, you didn't have to see anyone else and they didn't have to see you.

Hillary's mom drank and smoked, and Hillary had horrible panic attacks. She even developed an ulcer when she was in seventh grade. Her dad wasn't dead like mine was. He lived in Springfield and had gotten remarried. When he and her mom split, he had the marriage annulled, effectively erasing Hope and Hillary's existence. When we were fifteen, we learned that her dad's wife was having a baby. Mary Katherine was her daddy's new little girl, and his new wife wanted nothing to do with Hillary or Hope.

When Hillary was at my house, we'd sit in my room and talk about boys or about what we wanted to do when we grew up. I wanted to be a writer. Hillary wanted to work with horses. We styled our hair, and we did our makeup before going out drinking at night. When Margie would go into her room when Hillary was over, she'd call us "fucking lesbians," the worst insult she could conjure.

Sometimes when Hillary was over, Ma would tell us to go to Hillary's house and bother her mother. What she didn't know was that we could go to Hillary's house and really not see her mother at all.

\*

I never really knew much about Ma's childhood or whether she had dreams she was never able to realize. Hell, I don't even know how my parents met. Ma wasn't very forthcoming with stories about her life. When I was a kid, I asked a lot of questions about my father, but the responses I got eventually discouraged me from asking more. She'd say she didn't know or she didn't remember, or she'd change the subject altogether and tell me to look at the cat. I know that she converted to Catholicism when she married my father, so that means birth control was out of the question, which accounts for there being five of us. But I never really understood why she became a mother. She didn't seem to enjoy any part of it. I mean, sure, she told us that we were supposed to have kids because we'd need somebody to take care of us when we got old, but until then? Why have so many?

As I grew older and became exposed to more and more people who weren't abused, and I learned that my experience was not, in fact, normal, that many, many families were composed of people who *liked* each other and enjoyed one another's company, I came to see that my mother was, at her core, terribly insecure. I came to understand that she could not give me the unconditional love I needed because likely she had never been given it herself. This realization fills me, even now, with a combination of feelings that, together, make me want to just go curl up in a ball in bed because to articulate and feel them is so hard. Sympathy. Pity. Anger. Self-pity. Embarrassment. Shame. Sadness. The sense that I never had a chance, even before I was abused. I never had a chance. I wasn't going to be mothered even if my biggest wish came true, that I had been born an only child. I wasn't going to be mothered even if my dad had lived.

On Saturdays and Sundays when I was a kid, I looked through old pictures a lot. There was a dresser in my bedroom with two drawers filled with photo albums. I looked at them frequently, searching for pictures of myself as a baby. I never found one. My father was a photographer, and there were no baby pictures of me. The irony of this did not escape me. When I asked Ma why there were no baby pictures of me, she always replied, "Oh, they're around somewhere."

One day, looking through the seemingly endless pictures of Pam as a child, I found a tie-shaped Father's Day card made of construction paper. It was from Pam to Dad. It was signed "Love, Pamela March." I did some more investigating, found a letter from my grandmother to my mother, and put the pieces together.

Until a few years ago, neither Timmy nor Guy knew that Pam was not our full sister.

Timmy said, "She got knocked up with Pam, got married. She got knocked up with me and got married. She never wanted to have kids."

"She wanted *babies*. She loved babies. She just hates it when they grow up," Guy responded.

In one of the boxes from the attic, Timmy and Susie found an old Air Force yearbook and located a photograph of Lloyd March. He was a good-looking man, and it's clear where Pam got her round face and dark eyes.

*

When I was twelve or thirteen, Ma started taking me with her to ceramics classes, where she'd paint many of the pieces that hang on the wall at 73 Ferry Street to this very day. I remember painting a little Indian girl sitting on a rock, her red feather sticking straight up behind her head. Ma taught me how to work with the paint to do shading and texturing. It was just Ma and me those nights, and I loved it. I don't remember us talking much, concentrating instead on the work we were doing. Once, when I was away at college, Ma sent me a hippo she'd painted for me. It was a rare thing, Ma sending me something I liked without my asking for it or without it being a birthday gift. He's designed to sit on a shelf, two legs hanging over one side. I dropped him once but made sure to superglue him back together right away. I think that hippo might be the only spontaneous gift my mother ever gave me: conceived entirely for me without provocation. That hippo was evidence that sometimes she did listen to me. She had at some point listened long enough to hear me say that I really liked hippos.

*

She always had a hard time trusting others. She never believed that we'd do what we said we'd do or that our word meant anything. Hillary's memory of my conversations with my mother when I was a teenager is my saying to her over and over again, "Ma! I know!" in response to something she'd told me again and again but had no faith I'd either remember or actually do. She'd ask me to mow the lawn in the summer. I'd tell her I would later, when I got back from Hillary's.

"Are you gonna mow the lawn?"
"Yes, Ma. I said I would."
"When're you gonna do it?"
"I told you, when I get back from Hillary's."
"Awferchrissake. I'll just do it myself."
"Ma! I said I'd do it!"

A half hour later she'd say, "Are you gonna mow the lawn for me?" And the back-and-forth would begin again.

It never changed. No matter how many times one of us would assure her that we'd do what we said we would, if it didn't happen immediately, in her mind it wasn't going to happen. Such a habit bespeaks a lifetime of broken promises and disappointment, of language not doing what it's supposed to do. Language is emptied of its meaning when you can't believe that saying "I'll do it" means it'll get done.

It occurs to me now that Ma was never a very good promise-keeper herself. She'd frequently answer my requests with the words she knew I wanted to hear, designed explicitly to shut me up. "Ma, can we go to Mountain Park this weekend?"

"I don't know."
"Ma, come onnnnnn ...."
"Fine. Now leave me alone." The weekend would arrive and her memory would leave.
"But Ma, you said we could go."
"I say a lotta things."

As I got older, I became better at detecting when she was trying to shush me and I'd call her on it. "You're saying that just to shut me up, aren't you?"

"No ...." And a smile would slowly take shape in her eyes.
"I knew it."

Language, both written and spoken, has always been for me a kind of action. If you say it, it means something. The first time I say "I love you" to a boy, I experience the fear and exhilaration that comes with knowing that I can't take it back. Once it's out there, it's out there. The same was true for all the horrible things Margie called me every day. But Ma seemed to experience language in a way precisely contrary to this. Saying something aloud meant nothing. Language and action for her were two separate things. Words were filler, a way to get you off her back. She understood what we wanted to hear, and she was teaching us early that promises are empty, that words are hollow, that you can't trust anyone if all they give you is words.

*

It would be easy to say that Ma didn't try very hard to protect me, because it's mostly true. But I do have memories of Ma dropping me off next door at her friend Chris's house on some of the nights she would go out. So she must have heard some of what I was telling her. She must have heard some of my desperate fear that, when she left the house, Margie was going to kill me.

Ma didn't know how to fix the problem, so she removed me from the house, teaching me that the abuse was inevitable, and the only solution was withdrawal.

Resignation. Capitulation. Surrender. So very early on.

*

Money was always tight. We never had any. Ma had never been good at managing money, and for as long as I can remember, she lived from month to month, from social security check to social security check. Always at the end of the month, she was broke. As in, down to twenty dollars to get her through a week or ten days. When I was a kid, I'd sometimes steal quarters or even dollar bills from her wallet, and I often asked her for money. This was one of the things that drove my siblings nuts, that Ma would give me money almost whenever I asked. I was spoiled. This is why my only identity in my childhood home was a brat. I think she did it to shut me up. Giving me five dollars got me off her back for a while.

At the same time, Ma was a sucker for any kind of attention from a nice man, so when, during my last year of high school, a siding and window salesman stopped by the house and complimented Ma on her hair and asked if he could come in and sit down with her for a few minutes, she said yes. I came downstairs to see this man smooth-talking Ma into buying new siding for the house, so I interrupted him and told him that I was going away to college next year and we really couldn't afford new siding right now. Ma waved her hand dismissively at me as she stared at the nice man. "Oh, Amy," she said, embarrassed.

"Well? What do you want me to say? I want to go to college."
"I know you do. Leave us alone."
"We can't have new siding and pay for college." The salesman eventually got the hint and wished me luck at school next year. When he left, Ma said, "Wasn't he nice?"
"Yes. He's a salesman. He's supposed to be nice. And all he wanted was your money."
"Well I thought he was very nice."
"Good thing I was here. Otherwise you might be paying for siding you can't afford."

Not very many years later, Ma would insist that Margie's boyfriend, the father of her baby, the man who stormed into the house one day and threatened Ma with a knife if he didn't tell her where Margie was, was *nice*. I think he had sent some kind of fruit basket as an apology. The man who threatened her with a knife was *nice*.

Men. Stay away from them. Don't let them get you pregnant until you're married. If you do marry one, make sure he's rich. But beware. They could come after you at any time. But then again, their attention, even their shallow, transparently selfish attention, could turn your day around. Until your self-righteous teenage daughter comes along to ruin the moment.

*

I would not be like my mother with men. I would grow up to be a righteous feminist, refusing to submit to a man in any way, refusing to need one, to be with one who made more money than I did, shit, refusing even to be nice to them half the time. My mother's message about men being dangerous sunk in over time. Men were trouble, more trouble perhaps than they were worth.

But then again, some of them really were kind. Some of them really were *hot*. What the hell did my mother know?

Though there were other boyfriends before him, Michael was my first love. I can't remember what we did on our first date, but I do remember that first kiss up against his car in my driveway. "Do you want to go out with me?" he asked. I nodded. He put his hand behind my head and pulled me toward him. I tingled all over. I blush thinking about it now, twenty-some-odd years later.

Michael came from a good family—parents who cared, a younger sister he cared about and wouldn't dream of hitting. I was intimidated by the way they seemed to like one another. They seemed to like me, too, but I didn't trust it. I couldn't trust it. I knew Michael liked me because he was physically affectionate with me, but his parents were another story. Of course they could see right through me, what a bad and ugly person I was deep down. So I didn't trust them because I knew, without their having to say so, that they didn't like me.

Michael brought a cake to school to celebrate my seventeenth birthday in the cafeteria with some of our friends. Not long into our relationship, I had dinner with him and his family, and when his dad asked me what my favorite meal was, I said a hamburger. "I like a good hamburger, too," his dad responded. Then he asked me if I liked steak, and I just shrugged my shoulders. I began to resent his parents for having what my family never did. They had a pool in their backyard, and his dad made enough money for a comfortable living. At Christmas, I prepared my answer to their inevitable question. When they asked me what I got for Christmas, I'd say, with all the indignation I could muster, "A roof over my head." But they didn't ask.

We had sex for the first time in his bathtub. I learned that it was his first time only after the fact when he wrote me a letter telling me so. We were in love, and we had a lot of sex—at my house when nobody was home, at his house when nobody was home, in the park near his house. We'd be lying in his childhood bed, fooling around under the covers, when his mom would knock on the door and ask us if we wanted cookies warm from the oven. You can't make this shit up. Even in the books I read, moms didn't deliver warm cookies to their kids' bedrooms. We'd quickly adjust ourselves to make it look as though we'd just been snuggling and, sure, we'll have a cookie.

My relationship with Michael was like nothing I'd ever experienced up to that point in my life. He genuinely seemed to love me. My girlfriends probably loved me, but there was very little physical affection involved. Hugs were awkward. We told each other everything, but the physical closeness I experienced with Michael transformed me into a person capable of being loved. I became singularly focused on Michael. All I wanted to do was be with him because he made me feel good about myself in ways that nobody had ever done before. He was the first person who *loved* me. He wanted to marry me. I wanted to marry him. We decided we'd name our first daughter Caitlyn.

I began to ignore my friendships with Hillary, Niki, Keita, and Jessica. They responded unkindly. They thought I was pathetic for giving all my time to Michael, and I realize now they were probably deeply hurt. The problem then was that I had never imagined myself as a person capable of hurting anyone. In order to hurt someone, they have to care about you first. And while I knew that my friends cared about me, deep, deep down I believed in my core that I wasn't somebody others could care about. I was fundamentally unlovable.

I understand now that Michael's loving me awakened something I'd never before felt: acceptance just for being who I was. It's easy to see from the distance of all these years that I experienced transference with him; I made Michael responsible for loving me in all the ways my family never had. He became my everything. Friends at college told me we were codependent. I didn't know what that meant, but I also didn't really care all that much. All I cared about was when I would see him next.

*

There was never any question of what we would do. I'd have an abortion. Neither of us was ready to become a parent, and we'd just started college, I at Clark University in Worcester and Michael at Wentworth in Boston. Michael got in touch with a counselor on campus to help us sort through what we'd have to do next. She hooked us up with a patient advocate, Laura, whose job it was to help me get an appointment at Planned Parenthood and to help me navigate the court system.

It was mid-September when we figured out I was pregnant. I'd be eighteen on October 20. According to the nurse at Planned Parenthood, I couldn't wait that long, because by then I'd be in my second trimester and the procedure would be a two-day affair. Massachusetts law held that I needed either a parent's permission or a court order because I was a minor. I knew there was no way Ma would give me permission and I didn't want her to know about this anyway, so we opted to go to court. I remember so little of what happened except that somehow we ended up in a courtroom in front of a judge who asked enough questions to determine that I was fit to make this decision for myself. We made the appointment, and Michael withdrew the four hundred dollars from his savings account.

Two weeks before I turned eighteen, Michael and I rode the T to Planned Parenthood in Brookline. We sat together silently in the waiting room until my name was called. I went back alone, changed into a hospital gown, and waited. Two nurses and the doctor came in. It was a no-nonsense affair. There was no counseling, no pressure to reconsider, no attempts to shame me. Someone administered sedation, the nurse holding my hand asked me a few questions, I got woozy, and it was over.

"You're going to bleed a lot," the nurse told me. "You'll need thick pads for a few days." My biggest concern was my belly pudge. I hoped it would somehow go away in those few days.

She led me to the recovery area, where I drank ginger ale and ate crackers and slept for I don't know how long. Michael was there with me the whole time, holding my hand tight, leaning into me.

*

Michael and I never spoke about the abortion in the years we were together. Only his parents found out, and that was because they saw his bank statement and confronted him about it. He told me about this through tears over the phone about a month after the abortion. This only cemented my belief that they didn't like me.

After he broke up with me two years later, I told my friends about it because my heart was shattered and I thought he loved me and look at what we had gone through and how could he break up with me? I thought we were going to get married. The part about going to court to get permission for the abortion added a certain bit of drama to the story, and I liked telling it, and I liked the responses I got from my friends. They thought I was so strong. They didn't know if they could have done the same thing in my shoes.

I never saw it coming. There was no warning, nothing. I thought everything was fine between us. I'd even gotten a single room for my junior year so we could finally have more privacy when he came to visit.

He came to visit just that one time in that room, to break up with me during the first week of our junior year. He told me we had worn each other out. I remember those exact words. I screamed. I cried. I begged him to stay. He turned to leave after just fifteen minutes or so, and I jumped on his back, attacking him, begging him to stay, please stay. Please. I ripped his shirt from his back and gouged him with my fingernails. His back was bleeding when he left. I screamed at him some more as he walked down the stairs. I didn't care who heard. I was out of my mind with grief.

When, after seventeen years of feeling neglected and hated and ugly and unworthy, you finally meet someone who tells you he loves you, that you're beautiful and smart and he wants to pay all kinds of attention to you, for always, and you let down your guard enough to let him in, you have to go whole hog. You love him back, entirely and unequivocally. And when that love is taken away, when he tells you that you've worn each other out, you don't understand. You've never known love. You didn't know it could wear out. Like a rug that's been walked on too often? Like a favorite t-shirt, worn and washed too many times? You just didn't know.

When I told Ma that Michael broke up with me, she said, "Oh, he'll be back. They always are."

"No, Ma. I don't think he will."
"Mark my words. He'll be back."

It's funny to think now about Ma telling me to mark her words. It wasn't an imperative so much as a prediction. It wasn't so much about what we should or shouldn't do, as so many of her other sayings were, but it was about what somebody else—a man—would surely do.

But I knew better than to mark her words. Michael wasn't coming back.

*

My sister. Men. Intimacy. The past. Her past. My father's past. She told me again and again to keep my distance. She just didn't teach me how. She told me *to* but not *how*. Just stay away.

But also from her.
Get outta here.
Go chase yourself.
Go bother Hillary's mother.
Get out of my hair.
Go. Get.
*Get.*

# 2  Searching for Stories

Living without stories is not an option.
—Arthur W. Frank, *Letting Stories Breathe*

I cannot remember ever hearing my mother tell a good story. She was not a storyteller, and she didn't seem to particularly enjoy other people's stories. She didn't read me stories before bed each night when I was young, though she didn't discourage my love for reading once I learned from my first-grade teacher. She and I would drive up to the Lewis and Clark Drugstore once a month so she could buy her magazines—*Cosmo, Ladies' Home Journal, Redbook*—and she would usually let me get a paperback book or a magazine of my own. Later I'd see her sitting in her chair at the kitchen table, flipping through the magazines, but she rarely paused for very long on any one page. I'm not sure she read the magazines so much as she looked at them. She watched plenty of television, especially soap operas, so she presumably followed the stories of the characters, with their dramatic relationships and deaths and resurrections following mysterious illnesses and accidents, but she didn't talk about them, at least as far as I could tell. Maybe she did and I just never heard her. But I can say this with some degree of certainty: my relationship with Ma was not built on stories. She didn't tell me stories about her life, I didn't tell her stories about mine, and neither of us asked the other to do so. It was only when she slipped into old age that I began asking her about her childhood, her hopes and dreams, but even then she answered largely in the form of short, unelaborated sentences. "Oh, come on. I don't remember!" My asking her for stories, even once I was an adult and she was elderly, her health compromised, was taken as an affront.

Ma rarely offered up information unsolicited. It wasn't, for instance, until I was twenty-eight years old that I learned the rather violent circumstances of my birth. My right shoulder, which had bothered me for years, was still bothering me, and one day I must have been complaining about it repeatedly, enough for her to notice. And that's when she told me that when I was born, the doctors had had to break my shoulder to get me out because I was so big. Ten pounds, fourteen ounces. Knowing this about my shoulder cast a new light on Ma's reaction when, in second grade, I came home with a note from the nurse telling Ma that I might have scoliosis. They'd done exams at school and noticed with some degree of alarm that I had a crooked back. "You're not crooked, for Chrissakes," she said when I echoed the school nurse's alarm. The rest of that silent story went: You're not crooked, you're broken.

I did seem sort of uneven.

I read stories all the time, and my friends and I probably made up stories and shared stories from our days when we got together after school. Hillary and I built up a storehouse of shared stories, ones we still look back on to this day. But in that yellow house on Ferry Street, there were no stories.

For a very long time I was under the impression that one of the reasons, if not *the* reason I came to specialize in the field of rhetoric and composition was that I've been for so long preoccupied with the concept of *belief*. How do we come to believe the things we believe? Why do we believe some things over others? And I attributed this preoccupation to the fundamental problem of my developmental years: my mother and my siblings, the people in my life most responsible for my well-being and safety, did not believe me when I told them that Margie was beating me up regularly. They shrugged it off, called it sibling rivalry, assumed I was overreacting, or just didn't want to deal with it. They didn't want to hear me. Ma told me to stay away from her and she'd leave me alone. I wanted to believe her, but the evidence suggested otherwise. Even as I grew into adulthood and I tried to talk with Sue or Guy about the effects of Margie's abuse on me, they were hard-pressed to remember that it was really all that bad. *They were there, in the same house, and they didn't believe me.* It could be no wonder that I would be drawn to theories of persuasion.

But Ma *did* believe me, at least some of the time. Otherwise she wouldn't have told me to stay away from her. Otherwise she wouldn't have dropped me next door at the neighbors' house when she went out for the evening.

I think I'm coming to an understanding of where so many of our beliefs come from at the same time that I'm coming to an understanding of why I'm drawn to the work I'm drawn to. In rhetoric and composition, stories are suspect. Narrative has long been understood as a simplistic genre, a way to ease students into an introductory writing course, perhaps, but not a genre worthy of its own attention. Much of my work as a scholar in this field has aimed to challenge this belief, and I'm not sure how successful I've been, though I'm no longer interested in engaging in that kind of work. What kills me is that I can say, "Narrative is persuasive," and critics might respond with *anecdotes* about why narrative is less critical, less scholarly, less well, *smart*, than what we've come to think of as traditional scholarship. Persuasive indeed.

Our beliefs come from stories. Stories persuade us what to value, what not to value, how to see, and how to ignore. "People need terms of *selection*—what to pay attention to—and following immediately is the need for *evaluation*, or what to think about what has been selected," writes sociologist Arthur Frank in *Letting Stories Breathe*. "Stories work as people's *selection/evaluation* system" (46). One way to think about the work we do in rhetoric and composition is exactly this: bringing to conscious attention our selection/evaluation systems. Bringing to conscious attention the stories that guide our thinking, for as Frank puts it, "people not only think *about* stories; far more consequentially, people think *with* stories. Or, stories give people their first system for thinking" (47). For people who grew up in homes filled with stories, this understanding is commonplace. It need not be argued. It has become invisible.

Because I grew up in a home without stories, I have never been able to take this understanding for granted. There were no competing versions of the time one of us kids did something funny or the time Ma did something embarrassing and we all laughed so hard we wet our pants. There were no stories about any of us that were told again and again to the point that they became fossilized. There were no stories about extended family members. Once my father died, most communication with his family ended. We heard about them only when somebody was sick or when somebody died. There were no stories about Ma's family. The only thing we heard about Aunt Judy was that she never called and she never came to visit, for Chrissakes. There were no stories. There were six people under the same roof, surviving but not living. Because living requires stories.

If the most basic component of a story is that it provides structure in the form of cause-effect relationships, here is what I learned about cause and effect: If you stay away from your sister, she will stop beating you. But you can't stay away from her because you live in the same house and she walks through your room twenty times a day. What your mother tells you simply will not work.

Here are the only stories we had. People get sick. People die. Things happen to their bodies that you cannot prevent and they die.

Though I can look back now as an adult and see the connection between my father's smoking and his heart attack, as a child all I knew was that he had died of a heart attack when I was four years old. The only question was who had found him. The story did not continue after that. No stories of grief. The body goes into the ground and the bodies above keep on living.

Pam died of kidney failure brought on by pancreatitis brought on by pregnancy brought on by a man who later would not agree to pull the plug, which meant she suffered needlessly for two more years, for a total of five, before she died at age twenty-two.

My mother's mother died of emphysema.

My mother's father died of mouth cancer, "a horrible thing to see," my mother would later tell me when I asked her about it as an adult. That's as far as she would go.

My paternal grandfather accidentally drowned before my father was born. He was thirty-eight years old.

My aunt Stella, my father's sister, had multiple heart attacks, bypass surgeries, and strokes. We stopped counting and then she died.

One of my father's brothers—I can never recall if it was Curly or Norman—had Parkinson's disease.

My mother's brother, Raymond, known all his life as Pudgy, was an alcoholic. He died in his fifties.

My stepfather, Warren, died of a heart attack after he and my mother had separated. Ma told me that she learned about his death by reading the obituaries in the newspaper. Her friend Chris, the same friend who protected me from Margie when I was younger, had known about Warren's death but had chosen not to tell Ma. Ma told me this. I was a sophomore in college. There was much more to this story, but this was all I got.

I look over this list, and it occurs to me that the only vulnerabilities we were ever exposed to as children were physical. Emotional and psychic vulnerabilities were completely off-limits. They simply didn't exist for us. And yet that is where the stories are. How do people *respond* to the pain of others? How do people *go on* after losing loved ones? How do we come to *understand* loss? Who have I become? Who am I able to become now? Those are the stories that were never told, that could never be told. Because those stories require a different vocabulary than simple cause and effect. One thing leading directly to another. The body gets tired, the body wears out, the heart gives up, the body dies. To respond to those kinds of questions is to tell of human experience.

This is not to say that we didn't learn how to respond to illness and pain. We learned not to cry, not to ask questions, and not to trust our bodies.

I've become interested lately in the body of scholarship in illness narrative, largely because I have found that that is where some of the best theorizing of narrative is being done these days. A subfield of the medical humanities, illness narrative investigates the ways narrative *works* for people who need to understand their new lives, suddenly colored with threat in a way they never were before. Arthur Frank's work in this regard has had the biggest influence on my thinking; his work has shown me how to think with stories, but more importantly, his work has helped me understand the difference between disease and illness. Disease is of the body. Illness is the experience. So the stories of cause and effect that were told in my family—the stories of the body breaking down—were stories of disease rather than illness. They were stories of dis-ease and death. But more, they were indicative of a fundamental dis-ease with perhaps the most powerful aspect of story: Frank writes that

> among different speech genres, stories have the singular capacity to generate the most intense, focused engagement among listeners and readers. People do not simply listen to stories. They become *caught up*, a phrase that can be explained only by another metaphor: stories get under people's skin. Once stories are under people's skin, they affect the terms in which people can think, know, and perceive. Stories teach people what to look for and what can be ignored; they teach us what to value and what to hold in contempt. (*Letting* 48)

Stories get under our skin, and they lodge there, shaping us, defining us, propelling us forward. Frank writes that stories' positioning *under the skin* means that they affect the terms in which we "can think, know, and perceive," and to this I would add that the *under* is an important part of the metaphor that suggests a lack of conscious awareness of the work stories are doing. Like the blood coursing through our veins, like the oxygen feeding our brains, stories keep us going, but we're not always able to feel that work being done.

In *The Faraway Nearby*, Rebecca Solnit writes,

> Mostly we tell the story of our lives, or mostly we're taught to tell it, as a quest to avoid suffering, though if your goal is a search for meaning, honor, experience, the same events may be victories or necessary steps. Then the personal matters; it's home; but you can travel in and out of it, rather than being marooned there. The leprosy specialist Paul Brand wrote, "Pain, along with its cousin touch, is distributed universally on the body, providing a sort of boundary of self," but empathy, solidarity, allegiance—the nerves that run out into the world—expand the self beyond its physical bounds. (148)

Empathy, solidarity, allegiance—these are the foundations of family, or so I've been told. Empathy, solidarity, and allegiance are also essential to story. Essential to family, essential to story, and responsible for expanding the self beyond its physical bounds. In that yellow house on Ferry Street, we were bound to the physical, taught what to do and what not to do with our bodies, where to put them and not to put them, what not to do with them, who could hit them without consequence, and that the biggest threat to them was not violence but disease. Bodies were subject to cause and effect. Values, beliefs, desires, *emotions*, any vulnerabilities not physical: off the table. Too uncomfortable. Bring those up and you're likely to get hit.

*

I'm not there when my mother has the first stroke, but my brothers tell me she was looking all over the house for me. Timmy is the one who goes to the hospital with Ma that morning. We figure out later that she'd probably had the stroke on Monday night and then had gone all day Tuesday without taking her medicine or her insulin, and that's likely what caused most of her confusion. On Wednesday morning, Ma came up the stairs to Guy's room asking him what he'd done with the baby. She was very upset. Angry. He was half asleep and he didn't know how to respond. "Do you mean the cat? She's right here," Guy said, pointing to Ruby.

"No! The baby! What did you do with her?" she shouted back.
"Do you mean Amy? She's not here."
"No! You stole her, I know it."

That's when Guy knew he needed to call 911. "I'm pretty proud of myself for that," Guy tells me. "You know it's bad if I thought to call 911."

Timmy and I text back and forth all day, and that's how I first learn that Ma had been looking all over the house for me. *Talking to her is kinda fun. She is laughing that she's going nuts.* One of us eventually picks up the phone so that we can talk rather than text. He tells me he showed Ma a picture of me from Facebook and told her that I'm thirty-eight years old, not a baby. She'd been convinced Guy had taken me. She wiggles her eyebrows when asked, moves her hand when asked, and seems fine physically. Her blood sugar's fine, blood pressure's fine, but it's her memory that seems to be tripped up. She can't remember who Susie is married to. She keeps looking for the baby.

I'm the baby of the family, so it makes sense to assume that when she says she's looking for the baby, she's looking for me. But the picture didn't help. Reminding her that I'm in Illinois didn't help. In the months and years after this first stroke, Ma's anxiety over the baby would only escalate, never to be quelled.

*

The day after Ma is hospitalized for the stroke, Tim texts me to tell me that she's still in the ER. He's trying everything he can think of to light a fire under their asses to get her a room, but nothing's working. He's exhausted. He hasn't slept at all.

I'd told Hillary, who still lives in the area, about Ma being at Baystate, and she offered to go visit her when she was done with her classes for the day at Smith. She called me after she'd been there for just a little while.

"She's very upset. Hostile, even. She wants out."
"Does she know who you are?"

"I doubt it. I told her I was gonna go buy her some magazines, but she grabbed my arm like she didn't want me to go."

"Jeeeezus."

"She's gonna be okay. She's incredibly frustrated. She's just sitting in a chair in the ER. She's in a diaper and she's strapped down."

"Jeeeezus."

"I'm gonna go back and spend some time with her. What kind of magazines does she like?"

"Oh, you know, *Redbook, Ladies' Home Journal, Cosmo* that kinda thing."

"Okay. The doctor's gonna be here between five and six. Make sure either Timmy or Guy are here."

A few hours later, after Steve, Susie, Timmy, and I have gone around and around trying to contact Ma's doctor, the hospital's patient advocate, and Ma's insurance company, all to no end, Hillary calls me as she's leaving the hospital.

"Amy, what I'm about to tell you is gonna be hard to hear, but I think you should know."

I take a deep breath. Hillary almost never calls me by my name. "Fuck me. Okay."

"She was very combative. At one point it took two grown men to restrain her."

I say nothing.

"She hit me a couple times."

"Oh, god!"

"She's upset, she's frustrated, and she's confused. I think she thought I had the power to get her out of there, and when I didn't, she got physical."

The language of my people. I let out a deep sigh.

"I wish I could tell you that it's either her short-term memory or her long-term memory that was affected, but it seems like it was a little bit of both. I stayed until Timmy and Margie showed up and I told them everything the doctor told me, which is that she had a mini-stroke and the biggest problem she's having right now is with expression. She can understand everything people are saying to her, but she doesn't have access to the words she wants to say. She laughs it off when she can't find the language, but I can tell she's frustrated."

"My god. What would I do without you? Thank you."

"Oh, please. Not a problem at all."

"I'm sorry she hit you."

\*

My family has always been awfully quiet except when we were angry. Language in our home was used to insult, to degrade, to humiliate, to threaten, to express disgust and disbelief, but it wasn't used to stitch together stories that might tie us to one another inexorably. Paradoxically, language was often used to shush one another, to persuade the other not to tell stories, to not go on, to just let it be. To just shut it already.

The other story that Ma keeps telling following the stroke is that her parents have died in a terrible car accident. We try to correct her, to tell her that no, her mother and father died years ago. Your father died of mouth cancer, remember? "Oh, everybody keeps telling me that, but they're wrong. I just spoke to them yesterday."

She had always had what I thought was a particularly acute fear of getting into a car accident. Along with warning me about the dangers of men, she warned me about the dangers of driving too fast, of driving in the fast lane, of crossing a street when a car was coming a half mile off in the distance. She was the worst kind of backseat driver. As a teenager and a young adult, this drove me absolutely bonkers. I asked her more than once if she had gotten into some kind of horrible car accident when she was younger, but she always said no, and she certainly didn't want to now, so watch what you're doing! There's a car coming! So the story of her parents dying in a car accident made a kind of sense even though I knew that neither of them had died that way.

When I call her in the hospital after the stroke, she'll say, "Guess what?" and tell me about her parents dying in the car accident. I'm usually able to change the subject after I correct her, but the story of the baby persists.

The baby is missing. She can't find the baby. Somebody stole the baby. She needs to find a way to get the baby back.

"Ma, I'm okay, I'm right here. Do you mean me?"

"No! For Chrissakes, the *baby*. The babies are missing. I need to find them."

Sometimes the babies are plural. Sometimes there is only one baby. Always they are missing.

In February, I fly to Massachusetts to visit Ma. I rent a car at the airport, and Timmy's waiting for me at the house. Ma's still in rehab, and Guy's out with his girlfriend, so it's just the two of us. I can't remember the last time I spent any time alone with Timmy.

We make a run to the package store, where we get what Timmy calls my fancy beer—Blue Moon—and a fifth of vodka. I also pick up a couple lottery tickets. Why not? Then we go to the convenience store that used to be Lil' Peach to pick up chips and dip. This is what we eat in Massachusetts: a lot of chips. They're still one of my biggest weaknesses.

When we get back to the house, Timmy tells me about the boxes Guy found when he cleaned out the attic. All kinds of old photos, documents, letters, even, that give us a much more complete picture of this family that fell apart when our father died thirty-four years ago.

"Did you know Dad owned a donut shop in Granby?
"Shut up. No wonder I love donuts."

Timmy laughs. It's a deep laugh, one I haven't heard very often. "He put down fifty dollars on the loan for it. That and his camera. He put his goddamn camera down as collateral."

"Are there any pictures of the shop?"
"We haven't found any, but who knows."
"What was it called?"
"Granby Donut Shop." He laughs again.

We spend hours going through the photos. Our father was an incredible photographer. There are hundreds of photos of Pam. "He treated her like gold," Timmy says. These are all the photos I remember digging through as a kid, searching for some evidence of little baby me. We find Dad's honorable discharge from the Army; we find Pam's birth certificate with Dad's name filled in, which had to be a revision, since we now know that Lloyd March was Pam's biological father. We find Ma's DD-214, confirming that she worked as a switchboard operator for the Air Force. Timmy tells me that he's gonna try to get her Veterans Benefits now that he has this.

Timmy and I talk a bit about how Ma has always been so depressed. "Everyone in this family is depressed, I think," I say.

"Yeah, I finally went to see a therapist a few years ago and she made me think about Ma's childhood. I'd never really thought about how her childhood affected her as an adult." His therapist asked him how he was raised, and he realized, for the first time, that he really hadn't been raised.

"Oh, absolutely." We talk for a bit about antidepressants, I tell him that without them I'd've been dead a long time ago. "There's no way I could've been a teacher without them," I say.

Guy comes home while we're still going through the boxes. It must be 11:00 or so by this point. "You're going through these again?"

"I haven't seen all this stuff," I say.

"We've been through these boxes at least three times in the last few weeks with Susie and Crystal."

"But every time we find something new," Timmy says.

"'dyou find the contract for the TV yet?"

"Not yet," Timmy says.

"Yeah, what was that all about?" I ask. "I knew there was something about Ma getting the TV free because Dad died, but I don't know the details."

"It was something like, if you die before we deliver the TV, it's yours free," Timmy says.

"What the hell kind of contract is that?" I ask.

Guy shouts, "I think it must've been if you die before you pay it off, it's free."

I get out my laptop. "I've gotta write this shit down."

Guy shouts again. "You document this on your own time. We're just talking here."

"She had to go to the place with his death certificate to prove that he'd died," Timmy says. "Can you imagine?"

"Yeah," says Guy. "There was some kind of death clause." He looks at me with my laptop. "If I could type that fast, I'd be rich. I'm not kidding. I'd be stinking rich."

At one point during the week, I tell Guy I'm going to write a book about our family.

"The family's not all that interesting, Amy."

"IT IS IF YOU'RE NOT IN IT."

"Naaaah, we're not all that fucked up." Only a few years ago, Guy would've encouraged me to write about the family, to try to make some sense of the chaos that was our childhoods. What's changed? He's separated but not divorced from the mother of his second child, little Timmy, who stays with him at Ma's every weekend and every Wednesday night, he's dating Melissa, and he's moved back in with his mother. He's trying to convince himself that the family's not all that interesting.

He's been trying to lose weight for what seems like forever. He's got a little pouch and it grows and shrinks, but mostly grows, and every time I talk to him it seems like he's on a new fad diet. He tried the Atkins diet for a while and would eat scrambled eggs out of a bowl for two meals a day. He tried South Beach, he tried cutting out all sugar, he tried buying a treadmill, but the pull of the Doritos and the beer was always too much for him. This time while I'm home he tells me about a friend of a friend who's lost fifty pounds on Nutrisystem. "I think I'm gonna try it," he tells me.

"How much does it cost?"

"About three hundred a month."

"Jeezus."

"But Amy, that includes everything. All your meals."
"But no fresh fruits and vegetables."

He swipes, pushing the air in front of him away from his body. "Eh. Who needs 'em. I ordered my first shipment and it should be here in a week."

*

With Ma out of the house and the three of us together, we're learning things about our family. We're piecing together stories of her life, of our father's life, of their lives before they had us. Stories that will shape our own understanding of who we are and who we come from. Who we can be.

We seek ways to identify with the stories we find so that we can feel a sense of belonging to a tribe.

Frank draws on Althusser's concept of interpellation to describe the concept of narrative identifying. In all stories, characters are hailed, or interpellated, to embody a particular identity. Readers who identify with particular characters are thus hailed to embody those same identities. People are able to resist interpellation, of course. Memoirs, Frank notes, "are often acts of refusal" (*Letting* 50). As we learned more about our father's business ventures, Guy found himself wanting to identify with the version of our father who was an entrepreneur, opening a donut shop and giving up his prized possession, his camera, as collateral for the loan. If Guy found himself hailed by this story, he could claim determination and independence as qualities he'd gotten from his father. When Tim and I identified with Ma's undiagnosed depression, we could find ourselves interpellated in that story as actors who responded differently to our own depression, wanting to live differently.

When I read and read as a kid, I was consciously trying to mind my own business, to stay away from Margie, and to escape into completely different worlds. I loved stories that depicted families composed of people who liked each other—a kind of science fiction, I suppose. Strangely, I cannot remember a single title that I loved. I had no favorite book. I read a lot of Judy Blume and Beverly Cleary, but I read so much more than those, too. My reading was more than escape, I see now. It was an early effort to fill myself with stories, with possibilities, with models of who I might become. The only narrative I could locate myself within in that house on Ferry Street was one in which I was a picky eater or a spoiled brat. I needed other narratives. I needed to identify with and be interpellated by options my family wasn't offering. I filled and filled that aching empty hole inside of me with other people's stories.

Because I grew up in a home that didn't offer me stories, I had to turn elsewhere. What I was doing was reading other people's stories so I could create one of my own. In "Tricksters and Truth Tellers: Narrating Illness in an Age of Authenticity and Appropriation," Frank illustrates the concept of narrative resources with his own search for story. Following a heart attack, Frank finds himself in a bookstore, searching:

> I was in that bookstore because I did not have the resources I needed to generate a story about my life, as it had suddenly changed. Pretty surely, something had happened to me; I still have scars on my leg from scraping it when I collapsed during the heart attack, and I was gradually being convinced to take seriously the tracings from cardiograms. But real as these were, they did not in themselves make a story. Stories need more than events or evidence of events; stories are formed from other stories. (186)

*Stories are formed from other stories.* We build our stories from stories that have come before, and the stories we build become resources for others who hear or read our stories and draw upon them in some way.

In *Precarious Life*, Judith Butler points to an astonishingly obvious fact about human life: "that we can be injured, that others can be injured, that we are subject to death at the whim of another." But rather than lament the vulnerability of our human condition, Butler writes that it instead affords the insight

> that there are others out there on whom my life depends, people I do not know and may not ever know. This fundamental dependency on others is not a condition that I can will away. No security measure will foreclose this dependency; no violent act of sovereignty will rid the world of this fact. (xii)

In a society like ours, where individualism and autonomy are preeminent cultural values, interdependence will not be a condition we can see easily or perhaps willingly. Butler's concept of precariousness points to the differential degrees of dependence we attribute to others.

If we substitute *narrative* for *life* in Butler's theorizing, we can conceptualize narratives as socially dependent, as needing support from other people and other narratives lest they collapse. Butler writes,

> To say that life is precarious is to say that the possibility of being sustained relies fundamentally on social and political conditions, and not only on a postulated internal drive to live. Indeed, every drive has to be propped, supported by what is outside itself, which is why there can be no persistence in life without at least some conditions that make a life livable. (*Frames* 21)

To say, then, that a narrative is precarious is to say that its circulation *relies fundamentally on social and political conditions,* that structures and themes must be *supported by what is outside itself.* These are the narrative resources upon which we draw when we tell the stories of our lives. With no resources to support a narrative of, say, a young girl from a single-parent home growing up to become a college professor, that narrative cannot survive. It cannot be propped up.

If access to stories offers opportunities to figure out who we are and who we can become because the stories we create for ourselves are dependent on those narrative resources, recognizing that narratives are precarious should encourage us to tell the stories that challenge the dominant cultural scripts. Thus, telling stories is important not just because it is empowering or because it provides an opportunity for silenced voices to be heard or because it helps us develop form from chaos but because *our stories and others' stories are interdependent.* They work together to help us figure out who we can be.

And when stories change or when new stories come along, Frank notes that they then

> change the possible understandings of the stories that were its resources. Stories work retrospectively and prospectively: revising the sense of the stories that came before them, and also being resources for future stories that will, in their turn, revise the present stories. ("Tricksters" 192)

*

When Ma was in the hospital immediately following her stroke, Timmy noticed that her dentures were cracked in two. He called Aspen Dental, who told him that repair would take weeks. He didn't have weeks. "Come on," he said to the receptionist. He probably told her Ma was in the hospital following a stroke, and he just wanted to fix her dentures for her. And he probably laughed his big laugh. "Honestly, though, what do you use to repair them?" The receptionist reluctantly told him they just use super glue. "I got a three-pack of super glue at the Dollar Tree. Costed a buck! I'm good." The super glue worked. "I've got cheap running through my veins," he tells me.

*

For a number of years when I was in my teens, Ma worked at a factory in Holyoke making kaleidoscopes. She'd bring home small kaleidoscopes for us to look through, to turn slowly as we held them up to our eyes, watching our small worlds shift and refract and multiply.

*

The story of the missing babies persists throughout that first year. Timmy and Guy tell me about how Ma can't get past it, she can't be calmed down at times, and she simply won't listen to them when they tell her that there *is* no baby. In the beginning we all assumed I was the baby, a narrative that interpellated me as the child whose reappearance could calm her, the one who could comfort her in her time of need. Because I was the youngest and had the fewest restrictions and was given just about whatever I wanted when I was growing up, the narrative that I was the favorite child was easy to accept. But it wasn't working.

For a time they think she may be referring to Pam. This guess is given more credence when Ma calls me one Saturday afternoon—Ma *never* calls me, I'm always the one to call her—agitated and with *news*. She's on the verge of tears. "Pamela's dead." I tell her as kindly and gently as I can that Pam has been dead for years. "How come I didn't know about it?" she responds.

As most grown children of elderly parents in cognitive decline will do, I attributed her confusion to a dream: "Did you just wake up?" Or to something she was watching on TV: "Are you watching something scary?" Never mind that she had never been affected in this way by her dreams or TV as far as I knew.

I call her later that night to see how she's doing, hoping her confusion about Pam has been cleared up. I ask her what she's doing. "Nothing Just watching TV. Did *you* know that Pam's dead?"

The story of the demented parent is one that is told again and again because no matter how many times we hear it, we cannot get a grip on it. It doesn't make sense. It doesn't do the work it's supposed to do.

There are plenty of narrative resources at my disposal. But I resist them.

In her essay "Of All the Mothers in the World," Heather King writes of her mother's dementia: "Mom took a little fall on the stairs recently. And she's started to get belligerent (also wildly out of character: Mom's stubborn but extremely meek)." In "Love Sustained," Ann Patchett writes of her grandmother's slow descent into dementia:

> My grandmother, who had spent her life being easygoing, was becoming increasingly agitated. Bank statements and doctors' bills sent her into awful fits of panic. She would wait by the back door in the evening for my mother to come home and then wave the papers around tearfully, saying there was a terrible mistake and she didn't understand.

It's a story we've heard again and again. It's a story we'll continue to hear, but it rarely changes. Its precariousness is evident in our inability to hear it or to bear it.

"I find out tomorrow," Ma tells me.

"About what?"

"About the baby. What they've done with her. They're gonna tell me."

"Who is?"

"I don't know. The Brusseaus. They moved to the other town."

Guy tells me that when they're at the grocery store, Ma wants to buy baby food. He steers her toward the cat food instead.

A year and a half after the first stroke—and there were probably more mini-strokes in between—Ma was diagnosed with dementia. It was summer. Timmy told me about it on the phone. I knew she was declining, but I wasn't prepared for just how quickly it was happening. At the appointment where she got her official diagnosis, Timmy later found out that the fourth person in the room was there because Timmy was being investigated on charges of elder abuse. As it happened, Ma's friend Betty had reported him for taking away Ma's license, for taking all her money, and for threatening to kill her and the cat. Every time Ma saw Betty, she'd say the same things, so Betty figured there must be something going on and she'd better report Timmy to the authorities. The charges were of course dropped, and Timmy, to his credit, was able to see the situation from Betty's perspective. "She was trying to be a good friend," he tells me. I marvel at his patience and he tells me he's just worn out. He worries that he's on the verge of a nervous collapse.

I decide to visit again in November. She still recognizes me, and I realize in my surprise at this that I am conflating dementia with Alzheimer's disease. Alzheimer's is a form of dementia but not all dementia is Alzheimer's.

I walk into the house, the smell of cat and men and old woman assaulting me, the anguish and despair of these walls threatening to crush me as I put my bag down near the kitchen table. Ma sits in her chair at the head of the table. She doesn't get up, so I sit down next to her on the bench with its crusty layers of salt and syrup and Diet Coke. Her face is angry, disgusted, agitated. "I don't know why they're not giving the baby back," she spits out. "I'm gonna have to get a lawyer."

I take a deep breath. My heart is racing and I feel shaky all over as I tell her that I'm the baby and that I'm fine. I'm right here. I'm forty years old, I tell her. See? I'm fine. You don't have to worry about the baby.

She shakes her head, points her finger at the ceiling, and says, "Don't say anything about the girl. He doesn't believe she's missing."

We don't have much to talk about, so she returns again and again to the stories of her parents dying in a car accident and the missing babies. Nobody believes her and she knows it. It occurs to me that the first stories she's telling us about herself are tragic ones, and nobody's listening anymore because nobody believes her.

I visit with Hillary while I'm home and I ask her what's worse: seeing your mother's mind disintegrate if she was a good mother or a bad one?

Bad, for sure, she says, because it's so complicated. "It's not like she can say anything now that will make things right with you, and it's not like you can demand any kind of apology for the way she was when you were growing up."

When I talked with my therapist about my mother's persistence about the missing babies, he says the best thing to do is to figure out what's worrying her the most. Try to tell her in the vaguest of terms that everybody's okay and that she did the best thing for them. The assumption is that she's worried about their well-being.

*

One night I call Ma and we get to talking about her friend Betty. When I ask her why she hasn't been to visit Betty lately, she says she can't leave because she has the babies at home. When she said that, my heart sank. But later, after the phone call, I realized that she wasn't agitated while I was talking to her, and though she was still telling the story of the babies, they were *home*. They were with her. They were no longer gone, kidnapped by some unknown force.

*

Susan Griffin, in *A Chorus of Stones*, writes,

> Lately I have come to believe that an as yet undiscovered human need and even a property of matter is the desire for revelation. The truth within us has a way of coming out despite all conscious efforts to conceal it. (166)

*

Tim sends me a short video of Ma talking about the missing babies. She doesn't know how many there are, and she's not sure if somebody took them or if they're just lost, but that's not what's so upsetting about it. What's so upsetting is the lost look on her face. The scared look in her eyes. Her mouth wrinkling. She's on the verge of crying, and she has to look away.

My brothers are her caretakers now, and they speak for her, telling stories that she hasn't authorized. The explanations she's being given for why things are happening are all fabricated, evidence of the importance of the stories we're told in shaping our lives, even in the day-to-day. When Guy tells her that her doctor called and wants to see her, this becomes true for her even though the rest of us know that Guy called the doctor and asked if she could be squeezed in because her hallucinatory stories have gotten worse. When we're at the doctor's office and the nurse asks Guy and Timmy how long the symptoms have been bad, and Ma says, "What symptoms?" everyone just ignores her and Timmy answers the nurse. She cannot narrate her present life because the very symptoms she's there for involve faulty narration.

I tried again while I was home to ask her what she had wanted to be when she was a kid. She couldn't remember, or she didn't know, or maybe she never really wanted to be anything. There was no story there. Just whatever happened to her: that was her life. She had very little role in shaping it. But now, as she worries about her missing babies and wants, when she's at the grocery store, to buy baby food, nobody around her accepts this story. It's not right, this story. Nobody believes her, and because nobody believes her, she's doomed to repeat it until somebody does. But she wouldn't trust that we believe it even if we said we did. She has never been able to trust that what we say is what we mean.

*

After another particularly difficult Saturday afternoon phone call with Ma, I called my Aunt Judy, Ma's younger sister. "Is there *anything* I don't know about Ma that would help me understand the persistence of this missing baby story?"

Judy hesitated.

"There is one thing, but it happened a long time ago, and I'm not sure she'd want you kids to know."

Fearful that what Judy knew might make me even more depressed about my mother, I told her that I wanted to know *only if* she thought it would help.

"There was a baby that was taken away, but it wasn't by choice," Judy told me. When Ma was a teenager, she had a boyfriend that she was totally in love with—I imagine now this love being very similar to my love for Michael: desperate and life-sustaining. Things happened. She got pregnant, and her parents sent her away to have the baby. Judy was just a kid—there are nine years between them—and she didn't know where she'd gone. The neighbor girl kept asking her where her sister went and she had to tell her she didn't know! "I don't think she believed me. Eventually Mom and Dad had to tell me."

There *was* a baby. My mother was sent away in shame to give birth to a child who was then taken from her. Judy says Ma knew that Judy knew, but they never once talked about it. "Do you think she talked to *anyone* about it?" I ask Judy.

"I really have no idea. I doubt it."

There was a baby. There was a baby. There was a baby.

There was a baby.

The story she had been telling for months was not just a story, not something her demented mind had created the way it had created the story of her parents dying in a car accident. The story of the baby was true, and I wasn't the baby she was looking for.

I wasn't the baby she was looking for.

And just like that, a huge part of the narrative upon which I'd built my understanding of myself collapsed.

*

A 2014 issue of *The New Yorker* featured a story about a neuroscientist's search for her father's Holocaust narrative. Daniela Schiller's father, Sigmund Schiller, survived the Holocaust but never told his story to his family because he finds "being called a Holocaust survivor demeaning." The director Liron Unreich had somehow gotten Sigmund to agree to be part of a documentary about the Holocaust, and Daniela Schiller

> had explained that her father would never talk—that it would be a silent movie. Unreich was undeterred, and said that he was planning a trip to Israel, where he grew up, and would be grateful for the chance to film Daniela as she tried to engage with her father. Her father had no objection, so she agreed. "I told him not to worry, they were aware that he would say nothing." (Specter 48)

But he didn't say nothing. Instead, he told the story of his younger sister being shot from behind by a "humanitarian" police officer. "'He didn't want her to suffer, so he took her toy, threw it away, and said go pick it up. That way, he could shoot her in the back without her knowing.'" Neither Daniela nor her mother had known anything about Sigmund's sister. Daniela asks her father "if he had consciously suppressed this information."

"'Yes,' he said. 'You must suppress. Without suppression I wouldn't live'" (48).

I imagine that my mother would say something similar if given the chance. Without suppression, she could not have lived. And she suppressed that baby for more than sixty years. But her mind was breaking down, and thus so were her psychic defenses. The story she'd worked so hard to keep inside was seeping out. She'd been telling it to us straight, and we'd done everything except listen.

*

The word *collapse* was originally a physiological term referring to the breaking down or caving in of organs caused by a loss of support or intense external pressure. It's a falling *in*, a falling together. I'd always thought of it as a kind of falling apart.

When a building collapses, it affects all of the buildings around it. The same is true when a narrative collapses: it affects all of the narratives that functioned as resources for it and for which it functioned as a resource. I had lived my entire life believing that my mother was the kind of mother she was to me because of the twin losses she suffered when I was four years old. I believed that if my father had lived, or if Pam had lived, or both, I may have had a different mother. And of course that's true. I would have had a very different mother. But the losses to which I attributed her depression and her lack of care as I was growing up were only the second and third major losses of her life. The first one was a baby taken from her at birth when she was just a kid herself.

Because of these twin traumas, I have tried over the years, and especially as she's gotten older, to cut my mother some slack. Sure, she wasn't a great mother. Sure, she wasn't great at demonstrating love and care or even at protecting me from my own sister, but look what she'd been through. I'd be a terrible mother, too, if I'd seen my husband and daughter die within five months of each other.

But that story, that cause-effect relationship, has collapsed for me. I find myself, like Daniela Schiller, reseeing my own narrative. And my own life narrative cannot be separated from my mother's life narrative. As I put together my mother's narrative out of the bits and pieces she gave us through the years, I am forced to reinterpret my own. If, for my mother, giving birth was associated with trauma and a loss of control and grief and an understanding that a man got her into this mess but in no way helped her out, her desire that we girls marry rich men needs a new interpretation.

The story of my unhappy childhood caves in upon itself. It collapses. For it was dependent upon a conceptualization of my mother as one who didn't care, one who actively neglected me. But her baby was taken away. She'd been sent away in shame. She never talked about it because, as Judy put it to me, back then, nobody went to therapists unless they were crazy. "Back then, you were just a whore."

This is not to say that it isn't true that I had an unhappy childhood. Only that the beliefs that propped up that narrative have been compromised. And that I must somehow build a new one.

\*

Ma's demented mind is like those kaleidoscopes she brought home for us all those years ago. The two stories she tells us shift and refract and multiply as we turn them this way and that, never quite sure which reflections to trust. When she says *baby*, we hear one thing and she means another.

Shift. Refract. Multiply.

# 3   Witnessing the Collapse

> Sometimes the story collapses, and it demands that we recognize that we've been lost, or terrible, or ridiculous, or just stuck.
> —Rebecca Solnit, *The Faraway Nearby*

I was Ma's seventh child, not her sixth.

But I've always been her youngest child. Her baby. The baby of the family. Ma spoiled me. She didn't want to hear me cry, so she just gave in. I was so spoiled that I wouldn't eat a slice of Wonder Bread if it had holes in it. I said it was broken, whined, and got a new piece. I remember that.

SUE: "Ma liked having babies. Babies are dependent, don't think for themselves, don't talk back, and they need you. They're small and cuddly and they take naps. But I don't think anyone ever taught Ma how to mother kids after they learned to walk and talk."

When we were kids, Ma spent a lot of time on the couch in the front room, on her knees, elbows resting on top of the couch, looking out the window down Ferry Street. Sometimes when we'd be walking home from school, we could see her looking out, the curtain pulled back to the side. What was she looking for? Was she waiting for us to come home only to then tell us to go chase ourselves once we got there?

SUE, again: "Dad was not perfect in his parenting skills either. I remember that whenever we'd ask for something, he tried eventually to get it for us. We were spoiled! When we'd ask for something he couldn't get us (like the pony I would have nearly died for!) he said, 'Now don't I get you everything you want? Well, we just can't keep a pony here. A pony needs a lot of space and it would poop all the time and it would eat a lot.' Otherwise he would have gotten me one!"

Joan Didion famously wrote that we tell ourselves stories in order to live. Did she write anything about the stories we don't tell? "Let us remember," writes Claire Vaye Watkins, "that we become the stories we tell." To that I would add that we also become the stories we do not tell, the stories we cannot tell. Or do they become us? Do they undo us?

We often speak of the story of our lives as though there is only one, but of course, that itself is a story, a construction. There are so many stories of our lives, alternate versions that highlight this over that, versions that disregard altogether what another version might focus exclusively on. Our stories change as we do, as our perspectives and our understandings and our positions in life change. With news of my mother's first baby, the story of my unhappy childhood was destabilized, its structure rendered more complex, its morality less transparent.

The story of my unhappy childhood was a coherent and stable one, defined primarily by sibling abuse and parental neglect. It involved characters whose intentions were to make my life miserable because doing so met some otherwise unmet need of theirs. As I grew older and learned about the proximity of my father's and Pam's deaths, I tried to cut my mother some slack, as I recognized that I couldn't understand the suffering she had gone through in such a short period of time. I rationalized that any mother would be a bad mother under such circumstances. My father's death and Pam's death are what Sara Cobb calls contextualizing narratives, which

> thicken and contextualize the episodes in the main plot line, providing a context in which to understand or make sense of that episode. They are subplots .... They stabilize the main plot line as they provide context for understanding, for "thickening" the story. ("Stabilizing" 302–3)

The more contextualizing narratives, the more stabilized the primary narrative.

Pam's pregnancy at age fifteen was another subplot, one that functioned to stabilize for me and for Sue the force with which Ma would tell us again and again to find a rich husband, not to get pregnant before we found that rich husband, not to go behind the bushes with boys, not to bring any babies home because she sure as shit wasn't going to take care of them for us.

Moral transparency, too, is an important aspect of narrative coherence, and Cobb defines moral transparency as

> the explicitness of the moral order in the story, which, in turn, can be seen as reflexively related to the explicitness of the positive or negative value attached to character roles. The more explicit the moral order, the more stable it will be in subsequent interaction. (305)

The moral order invoked by the story of my unhappy childhood is one in which I am a victim who also recognizes the contributing factors leading to the creation of at least one of my abusers. I recognize that my mother was a product of her surroundings and of her circumstances, that she was likely in no way equipped to raise five children on her own.

What cannot be explained in this closed, unified narrative, though, is Margie. Her abuse of me. In the story of my unhappy childhood, the morality of her role has always been clear. She is a monster. There are no explanatory subplots that can stabilize a narrative in which it makes sense that she beat me for no reason and terrorized me even as I slept. She was not, herself, an abuse victim. That is one subplot that would help this story make sense.

I can intellectualize the story and say, as I did in "Learning to Keep My Distance," that Margie had the same mother I did, that she was terribly insecure, and that, in a home that disallowed expression of any emotion other than anger, her abuse of me was the only way she knew to express her anger. And yet. So many children who grow up in homes like ours do not turn to violence. There is no necessary link between the conditions in which Margie grew up and sibling abuse. There were four others of us who managed not to abuse the others. The narrative is not stable.

But this, like "Learning to Keep My Distance," is not an essay about sibling abuse. The morality of sibling abuse will likely always remain straightforward for me. Whether this is a moral failing or an intellectual or imaginative insufficiency on my part I may never know, but my softest, most tender and vulnerable parts cannot do much more with it. Christian Wiman comforts me when I begin to doubt myself in these ways. In his astonishing essay "The Limit," he writes,

> It did happen, though. It marked me. I don't believe in "laying to rest" the past. There are wounds we won't get over. There are things that happen to us that, no matter how hard we try to forget, no matter with what fortitude we face them, what mix of religion and therapy we swallow, what finished and durable forms of art we turn them into, are going to go on happening inside of us for as long as our brains are alive.

Violence is perhaps the most certain thing I've ever known. It has shaped me in ways I cannot articulate. It seeped into my bones at such an early age, into my marrow. It interrupts everything I do.

As I was saying, the story of my unhappy childhood was destabilized by the news of my mother's first baby. So much changes. I was her seventh child, not her sixth. But I'll always be her baby.

\*

When I told Guy what I learned from Judy about Ma's first baby, the first thing he said was, "There's *another* one of us out there? Poor thing."

Ma kept the secret of her first child for more than sixty years. But her body couldn't keep it in any longer. Her body was breaking down and the secret came out, but her body no longer knew it was a secret. Her body was just worried about her missing baby. Her body had never forgotten.

What happens to a part of oneself that is secreted away in shame? What happens to a story that never gets told?

Ma had always been something of a mystery to us, never revealing anything about herself, about her childhood, her past, her likes or dislikes. What we knew of her we knew only from observation. And what we observed, what she showed us, was frustration, anger, and a desire to get away, either by staring blankly at the television or by driving herself down to Enfield, Connecticut, twice a week to go to "the dance," where she would meet new men who would give her the kind of attention we couldn't.

As I write, I keep finding myself resisting the telling of what I know about my mother's first baby. It's not much, what I know, but the reverberations are huge and so I find myself wanting to put it off, the confrontation with the truth, the implications of the fact of the baby for my story, for my mother's story, for my family's story. And yet that's why I'm writing these essays in the first place: to do this work of recovery, to try to bring to light what has for so long remained in the dark, to try to come to terms with the work of narrative in life— the work we know and the work we don't know. We are all, each of us, actors in narratives we didn't choose, narratives we did not and cannot author, and my mother's story and my story perhaps make these truths clear in ways that may bring others pause. We like to believe that narrative agency is simply a matter of choosing to tell our own stories. But narrative has agency over us, we are actors in narratives we did not choose and cannot control, and there are stories that work on us in ways we may never know.

According to Ann Fessler, between 1945 and 1973, "one and a half million babies were relinquished for nonfamily or unrelated adoptions" (8). We are the stories we tell about ourselves, and the possibilities for such stories are taught to us from an early age. "The girls who went away," Fessler writes, "were told by family members, social-service agencies, and clergy that relinquishing their child for adoption was the only acceptable option. It would preserve their reputation and save both mother and child from a lifetime of shame" (9).

My mother became pregnant when she was a teenager, was sent away by her family to give birth where nobody knew her, and was forced to give that baby up for adoption. She told us this story again and again— first by pleading with us about boys and bushes and getting married to doctors and then, defenses slipping away, she told us the story straight— but because we didn't know, we couldn't hear her.

I, too, became pregnant as a teenager. But I had different options available to me in 1990 than she had in 1950 or 1951. I wonder now how she might have responded if I *had* told her I was pregnant, that I needed her permission to get an abortion before my eighteenth birthday. Would my story have encouraged her to tell her own? Stories, we know, beget stories.

Back in reality, I know, of course, that that would never happen. Ma didn't tell stories. Ma instead got angry. I know that we can deceive ourselves, that we can tell ourselves something for so long that eventually we believe it to be true. Can that happen with a baby born so long ago? Could she have pushed that memory so far down that it no longer existed for her *as* a memory? Was she no longer on guard against its reappearance?

For a while, Steve and I tried to search for my missing sibling online, but we know so little about her. I assume the baby was a girl because each time Ma voiced concern over the baby, it was always a she. We know that she was probably born in 1950 or 1951. Pam was born in 1954, and Pam came later, after Ma married Lloyd March in April 1954. That would make Ma seventeen or eighteen when she gave birth to the missing baby. We know she was probably born in either Connecticut or Massachusetts, in a home for unwed mothers, but that's so little to go on. We don't know if Ma's name was used or if the baby had Ma's surname, and to be honest, once the search became the slightest bit difficult, I gave up. I wasn't really all that interested. Siblings have never been a source of happiness for me; why would I want to seek out another one? Oh, there's a chance that I could meet this person, this half-sister, and find that we have so much in common, that we like each other, that we could maybe build a relationship. Just like in the movies. In fact, if this were a Lifetime movie, that's exactly what would happen. With a little more grit and determination, I would find a way to meet my sister, who would be sixty-five or sixty-six by now, and we would immediately hit it off. We would look alike, talk alike, and have some of the same interests. She would be smart like me. And we would both laugh loudly together at something and we would stop, turn to one another slowly, spooked by how alike we sounded.

I have always had a very loud laugh. Ma, too.

But Lifetime movies are not real life. It's better this way. Some part of me just knows that it is.

*

All of us, when we tell any kind of story, draw on narrative resources, and the stories we are able to tell then become resources for other people's stories. Among the most widely used resources are dominant cultural scripts, shaped by dominant moral ideologies, such as, for instance, the narrative that an unmarried teenager who gives birth is nothing but a whore. This was a readily available narrative resource when my mother gave birth to her first child. Back then, Judy told me, nobody went to a therapist to talk about these things. Back then, you were just a whore.

As I digested the news of my mother's first baby, I had to reinterpret so many of the things she said to me while I was growing up. Could it be that those things she told me about men were her way of telling me her story? She was telling me her story slant, but I couldn't recognize it. I heard her words only as admonitions, warnings, and petty complaints. But they were her life story. In disguise.

It was culturally acceptable for Ma to say to me, "Marry a rich man when you grow up." It was culturally acceptable for Ma to say to me, "Don't have kids until you get married." To say, "Be careful what you wish for," or "Jesus Christ, he's ugly." It was okay for her to tell me that men were trouble because you were dependent on them, that they'd always come crawling back, that it was okay to cheat on them—hell, it was even okay to bring your teenage daughter to meet the man you were cheating on your husband with. It was okay to tell me all of these things because none of them challenged any of the dominant narratives through which she imagined her life. She would never tell me about Lloyd March or about her first baby because to tell me about them would be to tell me that she had broken the rules, that she didn't even follow her *own* rules. To tell me about them would be to categorize herself as a hypocrite.

And yet. As she told me again and again to marry a rich man, she was telling me her story in a different way. Marry a rich man, because you'll need money to raise the kids he'll leave you with. Don't have kids until you get married, because if you do, they'll be taken from you.

When I told her that I had met Steve, the first thing she said to me was, "Is he rich?" For a long time I used that moment to demonstrate how callous my mother was, how she cared only about one thing, and that thing was never me or my life. But as I resee her story now, the way she has told it to me through the years in ways I have never been able to recognize, that moment changes its meaning for me. It passes through the kaleidoscope, and I understand it now as her asking if he will be able to take care of me. I see it as her desire that I not turn out like her.

Don't have kids before you get married.

Have more than one kid because if something happens to the one, you'll be devastated. I had always assumed that this one was about Pam.

For most of my life, my mother was telling me her story and it went something like, I suffered a terrible loss and I don't want you to experience that kind of pain. I'll tell you what to do and what not to do, but I'll never teach you where those edicts come from.

Ma drew on the narrative resources without ever telling the stories. She pulled from them the lessons they made available and left it at that. She left a gaping hole I've been trying to fill for most of my life.

*

You need to have kids to care for you when you're old.

While my story was *de*stabilized with news of this first baby, *her* story was stabilized. The things she said to us all our lives slowly came to make some sense. They had a new contextualizing subplot that helped us even make sense of her fear and anxiety now, as her mind disintegrated, loosening its tight hold on the secret she had kept for sixty-five years.

Timmy was Ma's primary caretaker at home for more than three years. He worked a full-time job at the post office, using every sick day and vacation day he had for Ma's doctor appointments or to stay home with her when she was having a particularly bad day. Timmy had always been my big brother who hadn't cared much. He was quiet, a drinker and a smoker. He loved his Harley. He'd never settle down because just when he got close with someone, he went and screwed it up somehow. When I was a kid and he was in the Navy, we wrote letters back and forth, but that was the only time we ever really communicated. When he began caring for Ma, though, we talked a lot more. And I saw a tender side of him I hadn't known existed. I overheard him telling her he loved her even after she'd just gotten done berating him for something, accusing him of something, performing an exaggerated version of the mean, insecure mother we'd always known. He tried to calm her, telling her everything would be okay, and once he settled her in her chair in front of the TV, he came back into the kitchen where I was. I was expecting an eye roll or a snarky remark but he didn't do any of that. He sat down and told me how exhausted he was. Guy didn't help nearly enough, he said, and when he did it wasn't something he could count on. So Timmy had to do most everything himself. "It took us twenty-five minutes to check her blood sugar this morning. Twenty-five minutes. Christ almighty." He worried about his own health. He thought he might have a nervous breakdown.

"I don't think they call them that anymore," I say.
"Well, whatever the fuck they call them, I'm going to have one. I can't do this much longer."

In early April 2014, Ma was rushed to the hospital with what Timmy thought was a heart attack. Turns out it wasn't a heart attack, that her heart was fine. Her blood pressure was fine, her diabetes was fine, but her brain. Her brain wasn't fine, hadn't been fine for a while now.

She was severely dehydrated when she got to the hospital, and they were able to fix that pretty easily, but twelve days later, she's still in the hospital because she cannot go home. Each time I talk with her on the phone, she asks me when she can go home. I don't know what to say, so I change the subject.

She cannot go home because her two grown sons have full-time jobs, and they can't care for her anymore. Even if they didn't have jobs, they're not trained to care for her. That they've done it for this long is itself a marvel. Timmy's girlfriend, Judy, who works at the rehab center where Ma went following the first stroke, has advised Timmy to tell Ma's doctors that she cannot come home, that they aren't equipped to care for her. This would set in motion the search for a bed in a nursing home.

And it did. She was set to be released to a rehab facility in Agawam, but then one night she was so upset and so paranoid that she hit a staff member, so now the place in Agawam won't take her. And no other place will take her. During the day she sits parked at the nurses' station staring at her shoes. She's stuck there because of her bad behavior. The thought of this is almost too much for me to bear, and I worry that I'm not dealing with it in a healthy way. I can feel myself slipping into a depression, a deep, heavy depression that I am afraid I will not know how to get out of. Timmy sent me a photo of her in bed eating, and in it she is so tiny, practically bald, so vulnerable, so clearly scared. I wish he had never sent it. I wish I didn't have that image in my head.

Ma feels like we've all abandoned her, that we've left her in the hospital to rot.

Ma has always told us she's felt abandoned. When we would go out with our friends, we were leaving her behind. "That's fine. Just leave me here all alone." When, just before I began graduate school in 2000, Ma and I traveled to Alaska together to visit Sue and her family, Sue and I could not have any time alone together because Ma interpreted it as abandonment of her. We didn't want to be with her. We were leaving her all alone and, "Oh, don't worry about *me*. I'll be *just* fine." I ultimately realized her biggest fear by abandoning her in Alaska because I couldn't take it anymore; I left for home a week earlier than I had planned just to get away from her guilt trips. She was then forced to navigate her layover in a confusing airport on her own. Though I felt a pang of sympathy for her, it was not pang enough to get me to subject myself to another six days of what I now understand was emotional manipulation.

At the end of April, the hospital finally finds a nursing home that will accept her. Coincidentally, my husband and I move into our new home right about the same time that Timmy drives his truck behind the ambulance that takes Ma to the nursing home in the Berkshires where Ma will live out her final months. Timmy tells me later that this night does him in. He spent hours in the parking lot afterward just sobbing. He felt so guilty for leaving her there. All the years of guilt she had instilled in him, the three years of tremendous effort he had put into caring for her at home, it was just too much for him. He had never been taught how to cope with such overwhelming emotions. None of us had. Instead we had been told not to cry.

Timmy later told me, when I visited Ma in the nursing home, that he hadn't been able to go back except for visits with her care team. He couldn't bear it, he said. "You've been traumatized," I said.

*

The personal essay has become my favorite genre to teach at the undergraduate level because teaching it has shown me again and again just how powerful it is to ask students to think critically about their personal experiences in the context of cultural discourses that conveniently label and categorize those experiences in ways that flatten and neutralize them. I introduce the genre to them on the first day of class by telling them that the personal essay asks us to slow down when everything else in our lives asks us to speed up, to be more efficient and more productive. The personal essay is different from the personal narrative in that it balances narrative with analysis and commentary, as I am working to do in these very essays. It occurred to me at one point while working on my mother's story that maybe she didn't have a story so much as a personal essay, that what she shared with us was part narrative, part analysis, and part commentary. The emphasis in her case would have to be, of course, on the commentary. But even if I granted that Ma told us her story in the only way she could—by sharing the lessons learned and repeating them throughout our lives like mantras—what she gave us still wouldn't qualify as an essay because the very meaning of essay is "to attempt." One essays to figure out what one is thinking, to figure out how one idea is connected to another, to surprise oneself with the truth about what one actually believes about a subject. Ma never wanted to surprise herself, I think. She wasn't looking to figure anything out except maybe how to keep us all quiet so we wouldn't ask any more questions.

For Ma, there was no question about the truth of her warnings to us that we'd better marry rich men, that we'd better not get pregnant before we got married, that we should have more than one child, that we should be careful what we wished for because we just might get it, that you're always in danger of men jumping out of nowhere and grabbing you. These warnings had become certainties for her and so issued forth from her mouth many times a day thoughtlessly and effortlessly. There was no talking back to these words, no questioning them, no critiquing them, no suggesting that maybe they weren't fit for every occasion. For Ma, these were the answers to problems encountered long ago.

And though I want to rail against this as I write, I realize that we all do this, if perhaps in different contexts. The example that comes immediately to mind is the policies section on my course syllabi. Each revision to that section comes as a result of a specific experience or group of experiences that have taught me that, for instance, it's really best if I simply have a no-late-work policy. The stories that motivated such a policy need not be shared with students; rather, they simply need to understand and abide by the policy. A more personal example: I have lately lost all patience for people in my life who do not hear the things I say. Too often lately I have found myself repeating myself or I find that I'm answering a question and the person who asked it has already moved on. Because of this, I made a blanket declaration to Steve recently: "I'm done with people who don't listen."

Step back far enough, and it seems that we do this with so many things. This is theory. This is pedagogy. This is policy. This process of extracting the general from the many specific incidents is what allows societies to function.

But it shouldn't substitute for the story of a life.

Only now, years later, can I see that perhaps Ma meant for her own story to serve as a cautionary tale for us girls. The problem, of course, was that there was no tale, only the caution. Amy Shuman notes that the "cautionary tale works by analogy, suggesting the potential similarity between circumstances but offering the listener the chance for a different outcome." There was a generosity in this move, this offering. Shuman continues,

> The listeners are invited (if not explicitly asked) to recognize the shared circumstances and are invited to draw a clear boundary by making a different choice. *The whole point of these stories is that recognition*. If listeners recognize themselves in the cautionary tale, they might apply the message to their own circumstances; this is the premise of the cautionary tale. (emphasis mine, 76)

Because there was no tale, only the caution in Ma's warnings to us over the years, we could not recognize any shared circumstances. We had little idea about any of Ma's stories, about anything from her past, so our ability to accept her edicts as cautions was cut off from the start.

*

Ma's maxims were stories stripped of nuance, character, action, affect, and blame. They were stories stripped of shame.

While, in composition and rhetoric, we have a vexed relationship with narrative, we seem to have a relatively unproblematic relationship with cautionary tales. Shuman categorizes cautionary tales as allegories and notes that "allegory in its most basic definition addresses the double meaning of texts that do not mean what they say" (77). To this I would add that cautionary tales are anticipatory in that they depend upon the teller's ability to predict human behavior, to understand human motivations. When my mother told me again and again to stay away from men, she did so with the assumption that she could understand how I would behave once I no longer stayed away from them. The cautionary tale makes no bones about telling us what we should and should not do, what we should and should not feel; it is hardly subtle. Further, the cautionary tale presumes a stable understanding of cause and effect.

In composition and rhetoric, we tell cautionary tales about the future of portfolio-based writing assessment (Condon); politicizing the writing process (Kahn); rationality as rhetorical strategy (Bizzell); the road to mainstreaming (Edginton); when blogging goes bad (Krause); the short and sputtering life of a small community college writing center (Getty); infusing disciplinary rhetoric into liberal education (Diller and Oates); the undergraduate research paper and electronic sources (van Hartesveldt); and reinventing first-year composition (Graham, Birmingham, and Zachry). We tell these tales because we believe that each individual experience is somehow transcendent of, in Shuman's words, "the particularities of both person and experience" (76). We tell these tales because we believe that we are not alone in our circumstances, and we believe that others might benefit from our experiences.

*

In her article, "When Bad Things Happen to Bad People: Using Disposition Theory to Explore the Effects of Cautionary Tales," Emily Marett notes that, though persuasion scholars have examined fear appeals at length, "despite the popularity and prevalence of the cautionary tale, its persuasive effects have received little empirical examination" (266). Marett is examining the field of entertainment-education, and the first two examples of cautionary tales she uses deal with unintended pregnancy. The first is the episode of *Friends* when Rachel becomes pregnant when Ross's condom fails, and the second is a *One Life to Live* storyline involving sixteen-year-old Starr Manning becoming pregnant after having unprotected sex with her boyfriend. The latter was a joint venture with the National Campaign to Prevent Teen and Unplanned Pregnancy.

Cautionary tales traffic in certainty. They do not live and breathe and grow, as stories must.

*

Ma screamed through the night, nearly every night. Her bed was equipped with an alarm to alert the nurses that she was getting up, because she rarely slept at night but would instead get up to wander and scream, in Timmy's words, "bloody murder." He heard it once, when he was on the phone with one of Ma's nurses. "It's nothing you ever want to hear, Amy. I only hope I never have to hear it again."

I cannot presume to know why my mother was screaming. I can surmise that part of it had to do with the terror of not knowing where she was, who she was, where her baby was. The terror of not feeling safe, of knowing nobody, of feeling completely abandoned.

Ma's doctors invited a psychiatrist in to see her a couple times a week. If only she had had access to such care so long ago, when it could have done some good.

I remember a telephone conversation when I was in graduate school. Ma had gone to her doctor for a routine checkup, and he had suggested to her that perhaps she was depressed. "Have you ever seen a therapist?" she asked me.

Excited, but not wanting to scare her with my excitement, I tried to modulate my voice. "Yes, more than once. They've been very helpful," I said. "Why?"

"My doctor thinks I might be depressed. He thinks maybe I should see a therapist. What do you think?"

What I really think is that I cannot believe she's asking me this, but instead I say, "I think that would be a good idea. It can't hurt, right? Have you been feeling down?"

"Maybe a little."

I tell her again that I think it would be a good idea for her to give it a try, but deep down I know her well enough to know that the only reason she brought it up with me was that her doctor suggested it and that the only way she will take the next step is to be encouraged daily. She sounded so vulnerable then. And I knew that my encouragement wouldn't be enough. It would have to come from her doctor. From a man.

*

In late July I travel to Massachusetts to visit Ma in the nursing home. It's hot and muggy. My stomach is heavy, full with anticipation and grief, as I walk into the facility with Aunt Judy. I'm feeling sort of shaky and need to use the bathroom right near reception before finding our way to Ma's room. Ma's not in her room, we're told. She's likely in the activities room, the receptionist tells us. Judy and I walk slowly. Neither of us is in any real hurry to get there. I don't know what to expect. I'm afraid of seeing her vulnerable and frail. My bowels rumble and twist.

When we get to the room, I scan it quickly, searching for the mother I always picture in my head, the one with her big hairdo and her striped or flowered top. We find her, but she's tiny, hunched over the table she shares with two other elderly women. Ma's hair is not big. Instead, her wig is askew, she's strapped into her wheelchair, and there are bits of her breakfast stuck to her chin and her chest. I grab a napkin and wipe them away and cry silently. I turn away from her because I don't want her to see my reaction. Judy has tears in her eyes, too. A nurse brings us both tissues, and I turn back to my mother. I hug her, tell her I've missed her, and she moans sadly. I wish I could tell her she looks good. I wish we had a long history of intimacy to draw upon now, when small talk just hurts. I wish there were animals to distract us.

On the second day of my visit, one of the nurses tells me there are guinea pigs in a different room. I wonder aloud why Ma hasn't been taken to visit the guinea pigs. "Any animal will brighten her day. She'd love it," I say. Hillary is here with me today. She is kind to my mother, willing to forget the way Ma talked to her when we were young. We again make small talk with Ma, asking if she's seen the fox that other residents have seen running in the hills outside the room's enormous window. The setting of this nursing home couldn't be more beautiful: in the Berkshire mountains, tucked away on rolling green hills. It's rained a lot in the past few days. I ask Ma if she heard the storms last night. "They were pretty loud. I love storms," I say. Her response is hard to make out in part because she's not wearing her dentures and in part because dementia has robbed her ability to articulate, so perhaps it's best that we're not engaging in conversations of any real depth.

During the silent moments, Hillary and I let our eyes wander to the other residents. Mostly elderly women. Some are painting small wooden birdhouses, while the young female aides provide color suggestions and animated encouragement. I have to stop myself from thinking about how much their language mirrors the enthusiasm one might find at a preschool. There are only a handful of men, one of whom I initially mistook for a staff member because he can't be more than fifty. Later Hillary and I wonder together what he's doing in a dementia unit. Ma's pleasantly demented neighbor has fallen asleep in her chair and her head is drifting, drifting toward the table where her cup of orange juice still sits. Noticing this, Hillary gently pushes the orange juice toward the middle of the table.

When it's time for us to leave, I make the mistake of saying as much, and Ma takes this to mean that she's leaving, too. "Okay, I'm ready," she says, placing her two hands on the table to give herself the strength to get up. But she can't get out of her chair because she's strapped in. She's getting agitated. "Awferchrissakes." I'm at a loss. I don't know what to say or do. One of the nurses, sensing this, comes over to where I'm sitting and engages Ma in conversation about the stuffed cat I've brought her.

The nurse tells Ma about her own kitties and asks Ma to tell her about hers. I quietly slip away, filled with so much shame and so much sorrow and just plain sadness that my mother could be so easily distracted by stories about cats.

On the third day of my visit, Timmy meets me and Judy at the nursing home entrance. We've got an appointment with Ma's care team, which includes her primary nurse, her nutritionist, her social worker, and the head nurse. Judy, Timmy, and I represent the family. Apparently these meetings happen every month. The head nurse starts the meeting with an overview of Ma's health: her diabetes is fine, her heart is fine, everything is fine except her dementia. The screaming is really a problem, we're told. It disturbs all the other residents. I ask whether the psychiatrist has had any insights about the screaming and Ma's primary nurse say that the psychiatrist has diagnosed her with depression. I respond that I'm not surprised. I'm about to say more, and here Timmy interrupts me. "I'm not sure if you know this, but she had two babies taken from her"...

In my mind, time stops here. When I tell this story to others, time stops long enough for me to say: I'm silently saying to Tim, *Pam wasn't a baby*. I want to interrupt him. Correct him. Tell him he's wrong. There weren't two babies. There was one. And there was Pam.

I look at Judy. She's nodding at me.

"She had two babies taken from her at birth and never learned about what happened to them. Surely that's the reason for some of the screaming."

I hear next to nothing during the rest of that meeting because I'm trying to make eye contact with Judy or with Timmy to say, in not so many words, *What the fuck? There were two?* I nudge Judy with my elbow. She nods at me, mouths the word "later."

Somehow the rest of the meeting happens. Something is said, I think, about trying to move Ma to a facility closer to Chicopee because Timmy's drive to the Berkshires for these meetings consumes half of his day.

We're in the hallway. I don't even know what to say. "There were *two*? Were they twins?" We're walking toward the activities room for a brief visit with Ma before we three go to lunch.

"I'll tell you at lunch," Judy says.
"I just found this out, too," Timmy says to me. "It's news to me, too."
"Christ, how the hell many babies *are* there?"

*

For most of her life, Ma's story was a secret, and secrets, we know, are conceptualized as objects buried deep within us, rising or being pulled to the surface for the occasion of a telling, rusty, perhaps a little banged up in the process of having been excavated from so deep within us. Except Ma's story flipped that script. Her secret had been out in the world for more than sixty years, living a life Ma knew nothing about, and all she wanted was to have it back, to have it return to her. What was literally once within her had left her, and she wanted it back.

I had been learning, in the year or so between the time I found out about Ma's first baby and the time Ma was admitted to the nursing home in the Berkshires, to reinterpret my childhood experiences in light of what most certainly had to be Ma's most traumatic experience. The traumatic experiences I'd been attributing her behavior to—my father's death and Pam's death so soon after—needed reinterpreting, too. What I and my siblings had to do was to replace the screen story over every-thing Ma had ever said to us—the screen story she had seen everything through but which we had no access to. Drawing on the work of Pierre Bayard, Arthur Frank explains that a screen story is one that filters our reception of all other stories we encounter. Using the example of Maxine Hong Kingston's *The Warrior Woman*, Frank writes,

> The injunction that begins Kingston's mother's story, *You must not tell anyone*, marks a rare occasion when the screen is spoken. The story of the aunt's pregnancy is never to be told again, and it might even be forgotten. But all stories that are told will henceforth be substitute objects for that story. Every other story will be a screen behind which the story of the pregnant aunt lurks, affecting how that story is heard. That original story need never be spoken, but it will always be heard by the one whose consciousness operates with or through that screen. Other people will be baffled why she reacts to stories as she does, as she herself may be, until the original story is brought back to full awareness, freeing new stories to be what they are, not a reflection that both conceals and perpetuates the original story. (*Letting* 57)

Everything Ma told me when I was a kid was filtered through her experience of having been sent away to give birth to a child she wanted but couldn't keep. In her mind it made perfect sense to tell us girls again and again not to get pregnant until we were married, to marry a rich man, that men were trouble, but also that men were necessary. Ma never told us why men were necessary apart from their role as financial provider. She taught us nothing about what it meant to love or trust somebody. I think she had lost her ability to trust anybody long ago, when she was a teenager.

The narrative of Ma's first daughter could have been that she was a mistake turned into another family's good luck. The corresponding story of my mother, then, one might deduce, is that she made a mistake that ended up providing a gift to another family. No. This is not a narrative that would have been supported by the cultural conditions of the 1950s. Instead my mother made a shameful mistake that would haunt her for the rest of her life. And the baby simply didn't exist. Erased. Forget that she was born.

Stories have power over us, especially when we keep them secret. They direct us in ways we may not always be conscious of.

The longer Ma kept the story of the first baby to herself, the more the story fossilized and, paradoxically, the more it changed. It fossilized because it had no chance to change in the retelling. Stories change when we retell them at different times to different people for different purposes. But hers was never told. It transformed, too, in its years of concealment. It became not just a story about having a baby out of wedlock and being forced to give her up, but a story about *keeping secret* the story of having a baby out of wedlock and being forced to give her up. By refusing to tell it, by keeping it a secret, she reinforced its taboo status and reinforced the very cultural narratives that had persuaded her parents and her that it wasn't a story to tell in the first place. "Back then," Judy told me, "you were just a whore."

*

The three of us—Judy, Timmy, and I—drove to a little diner for lunch in three separate cars, and before I put the car in drive, I texted Steve to tell him there were two babies and that's all I knew, but I would let him know as soon as I knew more.

During this time, I had been working on an essay juxtaposing the story of Ma's first baby as I had learned it and the story of my abortion. We had both gotten pregnant as teenagers. Neither of us could feasibly keep those babies. The choices we each had available to us shaped so much of what we would be able to do with our lives following that choice. Neither of us had to raise a child, but Ma had to bury a secret, one that her own mother had told her was shameful, one that would come out only when her mind could hold it in no longer. I did not share my decision with my mother because I knew she would not approve, and I was thus able to avoid any shame she might have tried to lay on me. Though the dominant cultural narrative about abortion is that women who have abortions live to regret them, my own experience tells me that there aren't enough stories like my own out there. My abortion during my first year of college made it possible for me to finish college and to eventually lead a childfree life. Having a child at eighteen would have derailed me in all of the predictable ways.

As I drove the three or four miles to the diner, before I knew anything more about the second baby, I thought about this essay. What would the knowledge of a second baby do to my essay? Where did Pam fit into this? Giving up one baby was one thing, but *two* babies? Were they twins and we're just learning this now? Would I have to revise the entire essay? Or would I just write another one and let the first one stand?

And how could I be thinking about an *essay* at a time like this? I shamed myself even as I knew that this was how I coped with overwhelming information. I imagined writing about it, sitting at our dining room table back home in Bloomington, Illinois, beloved dogs underfoot, surrounded by books and stacks of paper, random sheets on which I'd written notes to myself, and sorting it out, coming to see what I thought, how I felt as I wrote. It's the only way I know to integrate material into my life, to make it somehow real.

When we arrived at the diner, there was a long wait to be seated. It was a small place, quarters were tight, and we couldn't very well have the conversation I needed to have while surrounded by hot, hungry people on all sides of us. So we didn't say much as we waited for our table.

Judy is not one to elaborate. When we were finally sitting in our booth with our menus and our glasses of water, she told me that Ma had the second baby after she was married to Lloyd and had already had Pam. But it wasn't Lloyd's baby. As Judy put it, "He liked other women, and she liked other men," and she got pregnant. She went away again, to the same place, presumably, that she went the first time, and their mother cared for Pam, who must have been just a year or two old.

Timmy tells me again, "I just learned about this recently, too. It's news to me, too."
"Judy, are we gonna learn about another baby in a couple months?" I ask.
"I sure as hell hope not!" she says and laughs.

Timmy tells me that Margie would come over to the house when Ma was having a good day and instigate her. She would come into the house and say, "Ma, have you found the babies?" and Ma would of course get all upset and begin looking for them and begin talking again about having to get a lawyer and wondering why the people took her babies, and Timmy could do nothing to calm her. And Margie would just leave.

"You know that I have nothing good to say about her, right?"
"I know. And you're right. She's just awful. Mean down to the bone. I can't believe she came over *just to instigate* her."
"Well, she always went out of her way to beat me. That's who she is. It doesn't surprise me at all."

For such a long time, I understood my attraction to the field of rhetoric and composition to be in part a result of my family's refusal to believe anything I said when I was a child, to the point that my own life was in danger daily. I lived in fear for my very life, hearing always, "You're dead as soon as Ma leaves." *You're dead. You're dead. You're dead.* But maybe it's time to flip the question. Why would I have any reason to believe anybody in my world? Who in my world was reliable? Margie was. She and her abuse were a certainty. Ma told me that if I stayed away from her, I'd be okay, but that wasn't true. I couldn't believe her.

Even now, twenty-some-odd years later, Margie is consistent, still doing the same things she's always done. And the one time Ma tells us a true story, none of us knows how to respond because we've been conditioned not to believe her. And because she is not practiced at telling this story, the story of the babies she was forced to give up for adoption, her narration never evolves beyond fear, desperation, and anger. It cannot bring order to her chaotic inner world.

We all tell cautionary tales. A syllabus is really a story stripped. In my undergraduate personal essay course, I used to ask students to write four reading responses throughout the semester on any of the essays they chose. That policy has changed in recent years such that students are broken up into four groups, and each group is assigned four essays to respond to throughout the semester. There's a story there. Sometimes I tell it, sometimes I don't.

Point to just about any policy, any rule, any law, trace it back far enough, and you'll probably find that it came about as a result of a very particular story or set of stories.

Likewise, there is a relationship between the work I do, the way I write and the way I teach, and the questions that have pursued me for most of my adult life. My affinity for the personal essay, for its insistence on doubt and questioning, on vulnerability and attempting, on *trying*, is like the reverse of a cautionary tale. I am drawn to the personal essay's embrace of risk. Set against the cautionary tale's desire for safety, the personal essay's embrace of the unknown comforts me for it does not presume to know. It can only guess.

Later that night Timmy and Sue and I are sitting in the backyard of the house we grew up in. There is a fire in the fire pit Timmy recently built, and we're drinking beer and waiting for Guy to come back with the pizza. I wonder aloud whether Ma would've had abortions had they been legal then, and he said, "Oh no. Don't you remember the huge red bumper sticker on her car that said 'Abortion stops a beating heart'?" Apparently the sticker had an image of a tiny baby. She used to go on bus trips down to D.C. to protest abortion. I had no idea Ma felt so strongly about anything other than men.

Timmy also told me that Ma used to get very angry with Pam, who was a rebellious teenager. Ma hated Don, the father of Pam's kids. Ma used to hit Pam, slapping her on the face. Then there's this image: Pam sitting at the kitchen table, carving Don's name into her arm with a razor, the blood beading up slowly. "His nickname was Crow. What the hell kind of name is 'Crow'?" Timmy said. "What a jackass."

I have lived all these years of my life knowing so little about my family. With Pam especially, because there were so many photos of her, because my father obviously loved her dearly, I allowed myself to imagine that her relationship with our mother was somehow different than all of ours. That Pam had that Lifetime-movie kind of relationship with her mother. But Pam got pregnant when she was fifteen and then again when she was seventeen. She, too, had two babies as a teenager. And she, too, probably heard the same things I heard when I was growing up. Pam, the child in the middle of the two babies Ma gave away.

# 4 Narrative Fragility

> Each of us has a creation tale—how we came into the world. And I'll add this: Each of us has an uncreation tale—how our lives come apart. That which undoes us. Sooner or later, it will claim you. Mark you. More than your creation.
>
> —Michael Hainey, *After Visiting Friends*

I was Ma's eighth child, not her seventh.

When she had that first stroke in 2011, Ma was searching for the baby. "Where's the baby?" she asked Guy again and again, and he assumed she meant me, the youngest of us all. But she didn't mean me. She meant the babies that were taken from her when she was young, long before any of us was born.

She lost her first three children.

*Her first three children.*

That kind of loss is simply unfathomable to me and, I imagine, to so many people.

Rebecca Solnit writes that stories "can be both prison and the crowbar to break open the door of that prison" ("A Short" 19), and I want to pause for a minute on the metaphor of a story as prison. I want to think about my mother having been imprisoned by a story that controlled and isolated her year after year after year, even once she began having children with my father. The story of the two babies she lost to forced adoption disciplined her relationships with her subsequent children such that she had to, always, hold some part of herself back. As a prisoner would, she internalized the understanding that she was being watched and ultimately began to police her own language to the point that she would simply not talk about the past when asked. She would give vague responses like "I don't know" or "I don't remember," hoping that if she did this enough, we would get off her back. In fact, she often used this language with us. "Get off my back, will ya?" The accumulation of years of denial, combined with the isolation wrought by sharing the story with nobody, deprived her of a life. Ma could never feel free because she was always, *always* carrying with her a secret that threatened her identity.

The crowbar came too late, when her mind was no longer concerned with the prison bars.

Ann Fessler's interviews with hundreds of women who, like my mother, were sent away to relinquish their babies in homes for unwed mothers, help me understand some of what my mother must have been feeling. Fessler writes,

> Some of the women talked about the difficulty they had in forming strong attachments because they feared their [subsequent] children would be taken from them or would die. They stayed emotionally distant in order to protect themselves from another loss. (218)

One of Fessler's interviewees put it this way:

> When I had the first child that I raised, five years later—I don't know, it's like because you've learned this pattern of keeping yourself distanced, it's not so easy to break that pattern. So part of me always held myself away. Part of me always holds some part of myself away in every intimate relationship. I've really had a pretty hard time with intimacy, because it doesn't feel safe. (219)

And the shame that accompanied these pregnancies had to be overwhelming. As I think back on my mother's behavior throughout my life—her refusal to answer questions about her past, her silence about any aspect of herself, the absence of stories in our home, her mixed messages about men—I think about what Silvan Tomkins writes about shame, that it is "felt as an inner torment, a sickness of the soul" (133). Perhaps more significant to my mother's inability to experience joy or even interest in her subsequent children is Tomkins' articulation of shame as the affect at the opposite end of a continuum from interest. Tomkins writes, "The innate activator of shame is the incomplete reduction of interest or joy" (quoted in Sedgwick and Frank 134). That my mother still cared about those babies, that she was unable to simply let them go and move on with her life the way everyone around her expected her to be able to, caused her a great deal of shame. Shame that slowly, year by year, began to consume her, rendering her unable to parent the children that came after. She was hollowed out. She was unable to teach us, to discipline us, to protect us.

*

I was completely caught off guard by the news of my mother's first baby. It changed everything I thought I knew about her, and it forced me to change my interpretation of her actions throughout my life. If Ma was depressed not only because of the deaths of Pam and my father but *also* because of the loss of her firstborn baby, Ma was not just a grieving widow and mother but also a mother whose child was taken from her. As my brothers and I struggled in those years after Ma's stroke and before we knew the truth of the first baby, we listened to her say again and again that she'd lost the baby, she needed to find the baby, she would have to get a lawyer to get the baby back. Maybe sometimes she said *babies*, but it's hard now to say.

This reinterpretation, of course, forced me to reassess my understanding of myself. I found myself simultaneously angry with my earlier self for being so hard on Ma and willing to recognize that I could only know then what I had known then. I could look back and feel sympathy for the mother I had grown up with, but I could also feel angry that she had never chosen to tell us about our half-sibling. And just as soon as that feeling of anger surfaced, I pushed it away because it didn't yet seem like the time for it.

Ma lived more than sixty years not knowing what had happened to her firstborn daughter. She died without ever knowing. That kind of uncertainty is toxic to the self. And she shared it with nobody.

The uncertainty I lived with, on the other hand, lasted a couple years, and it wasn't constant. It was low-level uncertainty that I talked through with my husband and my closest friends and my therapist. My therapist helped me think about ways to calm her when she became particularly agitated. The thing to pay attention to, he told me, was what she was most concerned about. Was she concerned about the baby's safety? Tell her that as far as you know, the baby is safe. Was she concerned about the baby's well-being? Tell her that you know she did her best and that the baby is doing well. When I said these things to her, Ma responded as though I had told her the sky was blue.

My point, though, is that because Ma had never shared stories with me before, I didn't take her story about the missing baby seriously. And then I learned it was true and had to rethink some things.

Narratives collapsed.

Learning about the second baby caught me off guard, but in a different way. As soon as Judy told me, I could feel the judgment rushing through me. The cultural narratives I needed so desperately to resist. I could hear Judy saying, when she had told me about the first baby, "Back then, you were just a whore," and I could hear myself positioning my mother into the narrative of the woman who hasn't learned from her mistakes. But I didn't want to judge her.

The narrative was ready-made, and it threatened to overtake my thinking. It arrived so quickly. I had to do no work to summon it.

We live in narratives we do not choose and cannot control, Cobb shows us. My experience learning about the second baby shows me that we also interpret our worlds through narratives we do not choose and cannot control. And those narratives arrive for us unbidden, latching on to our surprise and our shock, making resistance arduous for even the most critical-minded.

I didn't know what to do with the news of the second baby in part because I was afraid of what I might find myself believing about my mother. The questions I might ask. Like, why hadn't she learned from the first one?

The questions Steve might ask. Like, why hadn't she thought to pass that second baby off as Pam's legitimate sibling?

It was a different time, I tell him.

Right. And those things happened all the time.

*

I returned to Illinois after visiting Ma in the nursing home wanting to do something. I called the Alzheimer's special care facility that I drive by every day on my way to work. I told the activities director that I had a dog named Wrigley who wasn't a certified therapy dog, but she was friendly and had a lot of love to give. Then I told her that my real reason for wanting to do this was that I'd just gotten back from visiting my demented mother in a nursing home that had no animals and all I could think of was how badly that place needed animals. But that wasn't entirely true. That wasn't all I could think about. I thought about how *fast* my mother had declined and about how I would never again hear her tell me I was getting sort of wide and about how my brother hadn't been back since he'd left her there because leaving her there had done him in. He'd been traumatized. I thought about how my mother would never leave that place alive. I thought about how little in life endures, about how little I had to talk with my mother about, about how little she'd asked me about my life over the years.

Alzheimer's is a form of dementia, but not all dementia is Alzheimer's. My mother had dementia, but she didn't suffer from the kinds of symptoms we've come to associate with Alzheimer's. Her brain was breaking down little by little, but she still knew who I was when I visited and she didn't ask the same questions again and again. What happened to her instead was that the secrets she'd guarded for most of her life began to leak out in ways that stymied those around her. We just didn't know how to respond to her distress about the missing baby, so we changed the subject back to cats or the weather. We did to her the very same things she'd done to us when we were young.

All of this is to say that, aside from what I'd gleaned about Alzheimer's through reading or television, I was unprepared to interact with Alzheimer's patients.

The strong, dense smell of urine assaulted me when I first walked in. People just get used to this, I told myself. There were all kinds of dogs there for the pet parade, and all the residents were sitting along the walls of the common area so that we could walk through with the dogs. Some residents were fast asleep. Some were alert and interested. Some seemed so together that I wondered why they were there. Dogs sniffed at one another, rested their heads in residents' laps, and begged for tummy rubs from those of us who could bend down to reach them. My head began to hurt from smiling so much.

A lively man patted Wrigley's head happily.

"What's his name?"

"Her name is Wrigley," I answered too loudly.

"You're kidding. Like Wrigley Field?"

"Yep. Actually her name *is* Wrigley Field. My husband's last name is Field, so she's Wrigley Field." I smiled at our cleverness.

"How old is she?"

"She's seven." Again, too loud.

"What's his name?"

"Her name is Wrigley," I said enthusiastically.

"You're kidding," he chuckled. "Like Wrigley Field?"

"Yep. That's actually her name. My husband's last name is Field, so she's Wrigley Field. We're big Cubs fans."

"How old is she?"

"Seven."

"Seven? She's a beauty. You really will never find anything better than a dog. What's her name?" He patted her head as I said something about going to visit some of the others. We made our way to a woman who was holding her hand out to pet Wrigley.

"Do you live in Canton or here in Danvers?"

"I live here in Bloomington."

"Oh, Bloomington. Does he live with you?" pointing at Wrigs.

"Yep, she lives with me."

"Does she sleep in your bed?"

"Yep."

"She must eat a lot."

I smiled. "She does. She loves food."

"Do you live in Canton or here in Danvers?"

"I live here in Bloomington." My head hurt. There wasn't enough light in the room.

What I'd imagined would happen is that the residents would pet Wrigley and whisper in her ear and she would give them kisses and they would smile and tell me about their dogs, the ones who had died or the ones they'd had to give up when they moved into the facility. This happened once on our second visit, when I decided to walk Wrigley around the perimeter of the home. A female resident was sitting on a bench in the hallway near one of the dining rooms. When she saw us coming, a huge smile broke out on her face. "A dog!" I walked up and let Wrigley get close to her. She patted Wrigley's head and told me about her sweet little dog who'd died a couple years ago. She was hoping to get another one, but each time she went to the shelter she couldn't find one she wanted. "Maybe next time," she said, still patting Wrigley. She leaned in toward Wrigley's face and Wrigley gave her a big kiss. This made the woman laugh and tell me about the dog she'd had who'd died a couple years ago. She was hoping to get another one, but each time she went to the shelter she couldn't find one she wanted. "Thank you for bringing her here," she said as I stood up. "I hope you'll bring her back again." I smiled and nodded. "Bye, Wrigley," she said as we walked away.

I broke my promise to the resident who wanted me to bring Wrigley back to visit. After that second time, I never went back. I wanted to be the kind of person who brings her dog to visit Alzheimer's patients. But instead I just had a headache that stayed with me for the rest of the day. And my mother still probably never got to see any animals. My desire to do something for others in situations like my mother's assumed a balance in the world that I'm not sure I believe in.

But maybe there's more. Maybe, by bringing Wrigley to visit the residents at the Alzheimer's residential center, what I was really trying to do was distract them with stories about my dogs. Though I walked away ashamed in July when my mother was so easily distracted by stories about cats, I have spent plenty of my adult life distracting myself from life's difficulties with stories about my dogs. Stories about our animals always elicit other stories, and these stories elicit laughter and joy. When my mother distracted me from asking questions about my father by telling me to look at the cat, she was trying to distract me from pain to joy. Except it was *her* pain, not mine. What I felt was genuine curiosity.

It saddens me to think about the ways Ma and I each used language to shush the other, she when I was growing up and I when she was growing old. One would ask the other a question, and she would respond not by answering but by expressing indignity at the very question. *How dare you ask me that.* Or one of us would respond to the other by shutting the conversation down. *Oh, I don't know. I can't remember. Things are fine.* There weren't very many responses because there weren't very many questions. Questions suggest interest. I would submit that we didn't know enough about each other to be interested. Perhaps more importantly, storied responses to one another's questions would be dangerous, for as Arthur Frank notes, "What stories do readily is attract other stories" (153). I wonder if the reverse is equally true, if an absence of stories attracts an absence of stories, if silence attracts silence.

The thing about keeping her story secret, keeping it silent, is that her ability to do so was dependent on other people's willingness to remain silent. On Judy's willingness to stay silent, to perhaps forget along with her. It was also dependent on her own ability to silence others' questions, to quash curiosity in her subsequent children. Her life would become a hazy past that none of us could ever know.

*

Logically speaking, the sympathy I felt for Ma when I heard about her first baby being taken from her should have doubled when I learned about the second. Instead, I felt my sympathy diminish.

When an experience is new, it can be frightening. So much of it is unknown. When you go through that experience a second time, it's a little less frightening because you know at least some of what to expect.

Did she love the second relinquished baby any less than the first? Had she learned, by that point, how to steel her heart against the pain of relinquishment? Or had her experiences with Pam, now a toddler, made it even more difficult?

Who can say? I have nothing to go on. All of my questions are predicated on the assumption that Ma felt maternal love for these babies and therefore suffered when they were taken from her. She was a teenager. I was born when Ma was thirty-nine years old. It's hard to extrapolate the kind of person she was from the person I knew her to be.

"She was always the pretty one," Judy tells me. "Always concerned with her hair. Me, I didn't care what my hair looked like."

Judy also tells me this: "She loved babies. When they grew up, she couldn't be bothered."

I remember being a kid and being told I was smart, and looking around me and seeing how my more attractive friends got more attention, and clinging to the knowledge that beauty fades but smarts last. This is how I comforted myself. I told myself this as a way to get through middle school and high school and, well, life, really. The number of times I've been told I'm pretty I can count on two hands, but *smart*. Smart is something I know I am. The worst insult I can think to call someone else is stupid. As I think now about my mother being the pretty one, caring so much about what she looked like, about the photos we found of her, the *sexy* photos of her emerging from a bath tub wearing only a towel (who took those pictures?), I wonder if she just didn't know what to make of us kids. None of us was particularly attractive. Susie looked just like our father, big forehead, very large straight teeth. Margie looked like Ma but not as pretty. I looked like Ma, too, but there was some of my father in me. But none of us could make any kind of claim to being the pretty one. And the biggest insult she could think of to call someone else was not stupid but *ugly*.

*

"When you look at the word *remember*, the opposite of remember is not *forget*, it's *dismember*. Chop, chop chop," Andre Dubus III tells interviewer Melanie Brooks. "*Remember* means to put back together again" (13).

Though we have many narrative resources at our disposal, we seem to have an inability to hear stories about dementia. I wrote in "Witnessing the Collapse" that the stories don't seem to do what we need them to do, but I think it's more complicated than that. We hear them again and again, and in their repetition, they seem to mock the very illness they describe. But they also refuse to allow us to experience the emotion that so many scholars want to claim for narrative these days: empathy (e.g., Keen; Anderst). As Kent Russell puts it,

> For all their pathos, each dementia story comes across as an individual tragedy. You read it or watch it or hear about it, and you might fear something similar happening to you, but you can't really *imagine* such a thing ever happening to you. Literally—dementia is unimaginable. We can't put ourselves in the place of the demented; we can't wrap our minds around what it must be like to lose your mind. Instead, you and me, storytelling animals that we are—we invent confident memories of our future.

A demented person's stories are dismembered. They are broken. They are out of time and in pieces. To *re*member would be to put them back together again.

Dementia is its own kind of prison.

Dementia narratives are particularly difficult for academics who see it in our parents because we've lived for so long with the belief that knowledge can save us. But what if it can't? What if, no matter how much we know about dementia, no matter how many stories we read about others' experiences, no matter how much we try to parse the differences between dementia and Alzheimer's disease, we are still left helpless against its power?

The cultural narratives about dementia refuse to distinguish between types of dementia, so that all forms of dementia are equated with Alzheimer's. Because of my mother's dementia, I learned that there is such a thing as being pleasantly demented, which suggests, of course, that unmarked dementia is itself unpleasant. I also learned about sundowning, which is the name for the acute symptoms some dementia patients experience in the evenings, as the sun goes down. My mother experienced sundowning and was most agitated in the evenings, was often unable to sleep, and would, when she was still home, be up in the middle of the night, opening and closing the front door as though she were looking for someone. Timmy was always afraid she was going to wander off. She would sit down in her chair in the living room for five minutes and then get up and check the door, wander around the kitchen, check the door again, and go back to the living room only to start the whole process again.

Ma never forgot who I was, but the number of people who asked me that question suggests that most people do not understand that dementia is not Alzheimer's.

Recently I taught a short Honors course on representations of illness with the goal of encouraging students to think critically about the effects of the simplistic prevailing metaphors and narratives we use to understand common illnesses and disorders. We spent some time discussing the differences between stereotypes and assumptions about illnesses as opposed to the lived reality of them, and a student pointed out that perhaps one of the reasons for all of these stereotypes is that we never learn about these issues in school. We learn about them only via their representations in movies, television, and books unless—and this is a big *unless*—we find ourselves or someone close to us experiencing the illness.

When I teach essays and memoir, I always paraphrase Francine Prose's observation that memoir always tells two stories: the first is the story that you're reading, and the second story, the one grafted onto the first, is that the writer has made it, has survived long enough and well enough to *write* the story that you're holding in your hands. How have others lived with and processed the threat of illness? And though our demented parents and grandparents cannot always tell their own stories, we can share their stories as a way of bridging the gap between the simplistic cultural narratives and the more complex realities of dementia. And when we do this, we can perhaps make the tiniest dent in prejudices against cognitive decline that lead to our telling ourselves that it will never happen to us. Instead, perhaps, "we can name the horror for what it is" (Frank, "Writing" 234).

We learn about illness by experience. And we want to know what others have learned from *their* experiences, so we go out looking, as Arthur Frank did, for others' accounts of their experiences of illness. We search for narrative resources. This is why illness memoirs and illness narratives are so important: they show us how others have experienced the threat that accompanies illness and they show us that others have survived long enough to make meaning from those illnesses.

We don't learn this stuff in school. Essays and memoirs bridge the gap between what popular representations tell us and what our experiences tell us. They are especially important because they are pedagogical in the larger sense: they teach us how to be, how others have reacted. They offer a model at the same time that they recognize that there can be no such thing as a model. Because of that second story grafted onto the first—that the narrator survived long enough to tell the story—we know that what they've written has worked for them.

And though we don't learn about this stuff in school, some of us decide to go *back* to school to learn how to interpret the experiences we've had, experiences about which we *know* certain things but don't quite know how to theorize. We want to learn how to think about and interpret what we have lived through, what we are living through. We want to talk about it in ways that make sense of what we know but also in ways that help others make sense of what they, too, might know. We want to work our way back out. To do this we need narrative. We need theory. We need modes of working and thinking that help us see the interplay between the two. We need the personal essay.

\*

It occurred to me recently that there is not a single photo of my mother holding me as a baby. I do not know what my first word was. I do not know at what age I took my first steps. Photographs are opportunities to tell stories. They prompt tellings and retellings of moments that might otherwise be forgotten. My mother, who wanted nothing more than to keep her stories buried, married a professional photographer. Early in their marriage, her new husband took hundreds of photographs of Pam. So many photographs of Pam smiling—some of her looking off into the distance, serious, but mostly Pam smiling. In 1962, the year Timmy was born, Dad made holiday cards. On the front is a photo of baby Timmy all wrapped up in shiny paper and ribbons. On the left is a drawing of a family, Dad carrying a Christmas tree, Mom carrying a bag of groceries with a turkey sticking out on top, and the little girl pulling the baby on a sled. "New Year Greetings. Ed, Marge, Pam and Tim." On the back is a tiny photo of Mickey, our cat, and in very tiny letters, the words, "A Mickey Creation."

My father went out into the world and captured other families' moments. He developed the film that would generate stories in their families for decades to come. In this way, he supported our family. And just as the cobbler's children have no shoes, the photographer's children have no photos.

I cannot remember my mother ever taking a single photograph. I can remember her having her photograph *taken* by others—even this was rare—but she was not one to savor the moment or to record it for future recall. The lives we were living were not the stuff out of which stories were to be made.

With Ma in the nursing home, Timmy calls to wish her a happy Mother's Day. She can't hear him and is told not once, not twice, but three times, by both Timmy and the nurse helping her, to put the phone up to her ear. At the third such suggestion, she says, loud enough to hear, "Well, it's not up my ass!"

When I called later that same day, all she could do in response was moan. A low, mournful moan that ate me up inside and prompted me to tell her again and again that it was okay, that I loved her, and that I hoped she was having a happy Mother's Day.

*

When I felt myself inhabiting the question *Why hadn't she learned from the first one?* after learning about my mother's second relinquished child, I was interpreting my mother's story from within a moral framework that characterized sex as moral delinquency, life experience as didactic, and repeat mistakes as evidence of character failure. Sara Cobb says of "mainstream" moral orders that they are reflections

> of the array of narrative themes that circulate in and comprise our communities. In this way, explicit moral orders ... are *already* legitimized in the culture and, precisely because they have the weight of the culture behind them, they are more difficult to contest and dislodge. ("Stabilizing" 305–6)

Eight or nine years later—I cannot know the exact number of years, for I cannot know the exact dates of when my mother gave birth—her sister Judy, my aunt, the one who told me about the babies in the first place, went away to a home for unwed mothers to give birth in private, too.

Stories persuade by analogy. The reasoning should go something like this: Judy saw what happened to her older sister when she got pregnant and was sent away. Judy could identify with Margie enough to realize that she didn't want to make the same mistake Margie made. Judy could reason by analogy: if this happened to Margie, this would happen to me, too. Yet she still became pregnant and had to suffer the same fate.

If only people worked as neatly as analogy.

My mother's mother had told Judy when she was just a kid not to tell the neighbors where her big sister had gone. In fact, Judy didn't know because her mother hadn't told *her*. Easier for Judy to keep the secret that way. My mother's mother instructed Judy early on that my mother's situation was one to be shrouded in secrecy, in shame, not to be shared, literally, with the neighbors. My mother's mother then, years later, sent her second daughter away in secrecy to give birth to her firstborn. I was able, recently, to talk with Judy about this time in her life.

JUDY: I lived with an aunt for a while, and then I went to a home in Hartford.
ME: Do you know if it was the same home Ma went to? And what happened after the baby was born? Did you get to see it? Hold it? Or was it just taken from you?

JUDY: I don't know where your mom went. I got to see the baby very briefly. She went to an adoption agency.

ME: And then what happened to you? Did you stay at the home for a bit and then go back home? How did you deal with it? It must have been so hard.

JUDY: I went to my grandmother's for a couple weeks and then I went back home. I had to wear a girdle to hide the bulge.

ME: Christ. And you couldn't tell anybody, right?

JUDY: Right. The father wanted to know if it was a boy or girl, but I couldn't tell him.

ME: Oh my god! That's awful. Whose decision was it that you couldn't tell him?

JUDY: My mother's.

ME: And did you tell anybody about it throughout your life?

JUDY: My husband and kids know about it. They all had the right to know.

ME: Have you thought about her throughout the years or tried to put her out of your mind?

JUDY: I think about her a lot. Wondering if she had a good set of parents that loved her. Always on her birthday. June 10, 1960. When I came back home, I used to take Pam everywhere with me and some people thought she was my child. I thought my family deserved to know. You never know if it will surface someday.

ME: Right. Like it did with Ma. Did she know about your baby?

JUDY: Yes she did. When she heard I was pregnant, she said, Jesus Christ! Her famous saying. I wish we could have been closer. I loved her to pieces, but she was always the pretty one and didn't like the way I lived.

Judy's mother forbade her from telling the baby's father that the baby was a girl. What was this, a form of punishment? What could possibly have been her reasoning?

Have you ever had the experience of realizing that you've held two facts separately about the same person for a very long time without ever working to reconcile them? My mother's mother sent her away in shame as a pregnant teenager. My middle name comes from my grandmother. My mother's mother and my grandmother are the same person. It was only recently that I consciously realized that my mother's mother is Gertrude Elizabeth, the woman who gave me my middle name. I had always felt a little spark of pride that I had been named after a family member, for so few of us kids were. But I hadn't stopped to think about the character of the person I had been named after. This is the same person who forbade my Aunt Judy from telling her teenage boyfriend that the baby he'd fathered had been a girl.

Obviously there was more to Gertrude Elizabeth than these naked facts. But they are what I have right now. And they are what are shaping my understanding of this story.

Just as Judy was in some sense analogical to my mother some eight or nine years later, all of us girls were analogical to Ma as we grew up. Don't get pregnant until you get married. Don't go behind the bushes with boys. Marry a rich man.

Each of you is a replacement for me.

Each of you is a replacement for that first baby.

I wonder if, when she was little, my mother played with her younger sister Judy and pretended she was her baby. I wonder if my mother ever thought about Judy as an analog for herself.

Interestingly, Pam, the child between the two Ma was forced to relinquish, became pregnant as a teenager—a very young teenager. At fifteen with Lee Ann and then again at seventeen with Kelly. Lee Ann, Kelly, and I played together as children, and I always thought it was neat that I was their aunt even though they were both older than me.

I wonder if Ma told Pam to marry a rich man, not to get pregnant before she got married, to stay away from the bushes with boys. Or did those admonitions come as a result, too, of Pam's experiences?

By Timmy's account, Pam was into drugs as a teenager, dating Don Burgess—nicknamed Crow—and just generally rebellious. I wish that getting pregnant didn't fit into this narrative of rebellion, but I'm not sure how else to script it.

The first pregnancy was a mistake. Failed birth control.

The first pregnancy was the result of a youthful sense of invincibility. It will never happen to me.

The first pregnancy was the result of hearing over and over and over again that she should wait for the right rich man to come along before getting pregnant. She would rebel against such strictures.

Or, alternatively, the first pregnancy was planned.

But what fifteen-year-old girl plans to become pregnant?

We all act within narratives we haven't written and we cannot control. It is most often difficult for us to see this until after the fact. But novelist and memoirist Jenny Diski's articulation of the ways the cancer narrative is already written for her is a stark example of this truth, one a person can see *while she's in it*. Having just been diagnosed with terminal lung cancer, Diski is astonished that her first reaction is *embarrassment*. As she writes,

> Embarrassment curled at the edges with a weariness, the sort that comes over you when you are set on track by something outside your control, and which, although it is not your experience, is so known in all its cultural forms that you could unscrew the cap of the pen in your hand and jot down in the notebook on your lap every single thing that will happen and everything that will be felt for the foreseeable future. Including the surprises.

Narrative works us as much as we work it, writes Cobb, and in the case of some illness narratives—cancer narratives, especially—we're able to see this work as we're in the middle of these narratives. Diski acknowledges as much when she realizes that, though she does not necessarily want to accept the cultural metaphors that frame the narratives of cancer in our culture, she also cannot simply reject them:

> I reject all metaphors of attack or enmity in the midst, and will have nothing whatever to do with the notion of desert, punishment, fairness or unfairness, or any kind of moral causality. But I sense that I can't avoid the cancer clichés simply by rejecting them. Rejection is conditioned by and reinforces the existence of the thing I want to avoid. I choose how to respond and behave, but a choice between doing this or that, being this or that, really isn't freedom of action, it's just picking one's way through an already drawn flow chart. They still sit there, to be taken or left, the flashing neon markers on the road that I would like to think isn't there for me to be travelling down. I am appalled at the thought, suddenly, that someone at some point is going to tell me I am on a journey. I try but I can't think of a single aspect of having cancer, start to finish, that isn't an act in a pantomime in which my participation is guaranteed however I believe I choose to play each scene.

Is it that the cancer narrative does work on us in ways we cannot control, as Diski claims here, or is it that Diski is at an age at which she is *aware* of the ways in which the cancer narrative does work on her in ways she hasn't written and cannot control? Would a twenty-two-year-old cancer patient respond in a similar way? How much of our understanding of the ways narrative works on us has to do with age and maturity (certainly not to be equated)?

When Pam got pregnant at fifteen, to what extent was she able to see that she was repeating her mother's narrative? Did she believe that she was doing the opposite because Ma had told her again and again *not* to get pregnant? Would she have been able, had she lived longer, to see that she had simply repeated Ma's story? How much of narrative repetition through the generations is a result of willful immaturity?

These questions make me wonder, then, if narrative collapse can only happen to us at a certain age. Had I learned about the babies earlier in my life, would I have been able to integrate them into my life story, to understand Ma's actions and reactions differently, or does the dementia color everything?

Of course I cannot know. Of course the circumstances surrounding my learning the details of Ma's trauma traumatized me as well, and it is virtually impossible to imagine how I might have reacted otherwise. But I'm wondering about the age at which our stories of ourselves coalesce to the point at which a narrative force from outside can cause something like collapse.

\*

Ma screamed as she lay dying. She screamed in her sleep, waking up other residents of the nursing home in Willamstown, Massachusetts, a sleepy town in the Berkshires. She died on a Friday night, October 3, 2014. Steve and I were watching the final episode of *Six Feet Under*— you really cannot make this up—when I got the call from Timmy that she had finally died. She had been lingering for days, drifting in and out of consciousness, screaming while conscious. When my phone rang, we paused the show, I talked to Timmy briefly, and before hanging up we each said "I love you," an unusual experience for both of us, but it was an unusual moment. After hanging up, I looked at Steve, and then at the TV, and back at Steve and said, "I guess we should finish it." And so we did. And it was a beautiful episode. Ethereal. Fitting in many ways.

In Massachusetts for the funeral, Steve and I stayed in a hotel in Holyoke. We ate many donuts with my family. Steve met my Aunt Judy and, at the funeral, Lee Ann and Kelly. I had such fun catching up with Lee Ann and Kelly—and Kelly looked so much like Pam!—that I asked the two of them to meet us for breakfast while we were still in town. We wanted to get to know them a little better while we could. It was such a shame that our families were so distant.

My mother's funeral had been something I feared for most of my adult life, not because I feared her death or seeing her dead body, but because I feared having to see Margie again as an adult. Timmy had told me earlier in the day that Margie had paid for the clothing and various accessories Ma was buried in and the way it worked out, each of us kids was responsible for thirty-three dollars, so I had to give Margie that money at some point. Steve and I talked at length about how to do this. We didn't want to give her a check because we didn't want her having our home address. I didn't want Steve giving her the money because I didn't want him picking a fight with Margie. So it was decided that I would just hand her a wad of cash at the funeral. Which I did. I walked right up to her, said, "Here's the money for Ma's stuff," shoved it at her, and walked away. I didn't allow her to say anything in response. I walked back to my husband.

Later at the funeral itself, Ma was given military rites and Timmy was presented with the flag. I hadn't expected this at all, and I was touched by the solemnity of it. I read something I'd written, and I felt as I did so that I was taking back my rightful place as my *self* in this family that for so long had tried to squash it. That felt good.

The next morning we met Lee Ann and Kelly at Cracker Barrel in Holyoke. We talked about Ma and about Pam, about playing together when we were kids. We asked about their dad, Don, and learned that he had been a bad father, only coming around every now and then. I knew they had been raised by his mother, that Ma had not been a part of their lives, and I apologized to them on her behalf. "I know she wasn't a good grandmother to you," I said. They were both so understanding, and I could feel nothing but shame. I wanted my mother to have been better.

I raised the issue of Ma's teenage pregnancies, for I wasn't sure how much, if anything, they knew about that. We talked about the horror of being sent away not once, but twice, and as we imagined what it must have felt like, how it must have affected her as a mother, how it surely affected the way she raised all of us kids, Lee Ann said something about having been raised in a foster home for the first six months of her life.

I dropped my fork dramatically. I want to say I splashed syrup onto the table because that it something I would likely do, but I cannot be sure.

"*What* did you just say?"
"I was in a foster home for the first six months of my life. I was born in a home for unwed mothers."

Just as time seemed to stop when I heard those words escape from Timmy's mouth in the nursing home—"She had two babies taken from her"— time seemed once again to stop. I was in some kind of time warp where once again nothing at all made sense.

"*You* were born in a home for unwed mothers? How is that possible?"
I grip my hands on the table. I probably hit Steve on the shoulder as if to say, "Can you *fucking* believe this?"

I do not remember how the rest of that conversation went. I know we had a good time, and I know that I filed away, in a different part of me, the information Lee Ann had just shared with us. Information that once again shed light on the mother I never really knew. I would put it aside for now and interpret it later. I would process it with Steve, with Hillary, with my therapist, but for now it was important that I simply be a family member and not a writer. Oh, I wanted so badly to ask more questions, to ask how she didn't *hate* my mother for what she did to her mother, to ask how her dad spoke of my mother, to ask if she ever resented Kelly for having been born to their married parents. For it was once Pam and Don were married, once Pam was pregnant again, that Lee Ann was returned to Pam. It was Kelly's very existence that was responsible for Lee Ann getting out.

But I didn't ask these things. It was too much in the moment. But I felt a kind of excitement in the moment, too, a feeling that comes with learning that there is so much more to a story than I had originally believed. It was almost *too* symmetrical. I was probably jittery from that point on, shaking my legs up and down as I am now as I write, excited about the possibilities that come with seeing the big picture, the shape of this narrative. The grandmother is sent away not once, but twice, to give birth in private. The child in between those two babies grows up to become pregnant as a teenager and she, too, is sent away to give birth in private. Where is the choice in any of this?

Lee Ann was born in 1971. I was born in 1972. *Roe v. Wade* became law in 1973. Lee Ann's was the last generation to be born in such homes.

*

Lee Ann was lost to Pam for six months. My mother's babies were lost to her for her entire life. Loss. "We lose things because we are flawed; because we are human; because we have things to lose," writes Kathryn Schulz in her stunning essay "When Things Go Missing." Schulz writes of losing things, of losing people, of the concept of loss more generally, and as I read I cannot help but think about the work it takes to *create* the very things my mother lost. She grew human lives inside her body. Where once there was nothing, then there was something to be lost. "We lose things ... because we have things to lose." We lose things because we acquire them. We lose things because we create them and they are wrenched from us, often in the cruelest of ways.

When we lose something, Schulz writes, we naturally want to know where it is, who is to blame for it going missing:

> In the micro-drama of loss ... we are nearly always both villain and victim. That goes some way toward explaining why people often say that losing things drives them crazy. At best our failure to locate something that we ourselves last handled suggests that our memory is shot; at worst, it calls into question the very nature and continuity of selfhood.

Curiously, only once Ma's memory *was* shot could she locate the loss that had haunted her all her life. And by locate, I mean speak. Only once her memory was shot could Ma speak the loss because her body was no longer taxed in the work of holding it in. She could let it go because she could no longer remember why she was keeping it in. She could no longer remember the shame.

Schulz continues,

> The verb "to lose" has its taproot sunk in sorrow; it is related to the "lorn" in forlorn. It comes from an Old English word meaning to perish, which comes from a still more ancient word meaning to separate or cut apart.

Ma and her babies: separated, literally when each was born, as each was cut from her body. Separated again, literally, when each was torn from her arms.

Separate: the word I misspelled in my fifth-grade spelling bee. I spelled it with an *e*—seperate—was bested by William Schreffler, and swore to never misspell that word again.

We are our stories. We are the stories we tell about ourselves, and the language we use to tell those stories is paramount. We sometimes feel whole and centered with a beginning, a middle, and an end, and we sometimes—perhaps more often—feel undone, done in, breakable, collapsible as we experience a failure of meaning.

Gaston Bachelard writes, "What is the source of our first suffering? It lies in the fact that we hesitated to speak … it was born in the moments when we accumulated silent things within us."

*

My mother never told her story. Her story was secreted away in silence, buried in shame, and I am here now, still learning how to tell the story of my mother, the story of her trauma, the story of my own trauma at having witnessed the collapse of the narrative I had built up of her in relationship to me. In the considerable literature on trauma theory, much has been written about the utter importance of telling one's story. Susan Brison, survivor of a brutal rape and attempted murder, writes that

> Perhaps there is a psychological imperative, analogous to the legal imperative, to keep telling one's story until it is heard. After the story has been heard and acknowledged, one can let it go, unfreeze it. One can unclench.

But Ma was, as we know, never able to unclench. She held that story in until her demented mind no longer understood that it needed to be held in. And then, as the story came out, those of us being asked to understand it were flummoxed.

"What then happens to the story?" Brison continues. "Do we inevitably wound others with the transmission of our stories? There is some evidence that trauma, to the contrary, causes more harm to others (for example, subsequent generations) when transmitted through 'untold stories' than when it is narrated (Bar-On 1995; Fresco 1984)" (110).

Ma's untold stories were her truisms, her invectives, her cautions, repeated to us girls throughout our lives. Marry a rich man. Don't get pregnant until you're married. Don't go behind the bushes with a boy. Men are trouble. Marry a doctor. (Rarely have I stopped to wonder about the effects of these cautions on my brothers, what they must have absorbed about their own gender.)

The one I keep forgetting about, the caution that comes to me now as I think about Lee Ann spending the first six months of her life in a foster home: Don't have babies because I'm not going to take care of them for you. I'm not watching your screaming kids for you.

I wish I could know more about the story behind that caution. But part of me doesn't even really want to know.

In her astonishing essay "Learning How to Tell," Lisa Schnell writes of her inability to mourn her infant daughter Claire's terminal illness. She finds herself literally imitating the physical symptoms of Claire's rare illness, and she turns to Freud to understand what was happening:

> I had not been able to put any distance at all between Claire and myself. Trapped by a diagnosis, I had not managed the parental transition to object-love, even this counterfeit object-love that Freud refers to, and my body was acting out the narcissistic predicament I found myself in. (269)

Schnell's reading of Freud's landmark "Mourning and Melancholia" reminds both her and us that "simply put, proper mourning requires the perception, or more accurately, the renewed perception of *space*" (273). She continues,

> Language is inherently representational; its very nature, in other words is to *stand for* something else—an object, a concept, a feeling. To use language deliberately, therefore, is an acknowledgement of space, of the cognitive distance between the thing itself and that with which we represent the thing. (274)

Schnell then turns to literary theorist Terry Eagleton, who explains that loss is necessary in any narrative:

> Something must be lost or absent in any narrative for it to unfold: if everything stayed in place there would be no story to tell. This loss is distressing, but exciting as well: desire is stimulated by what we cannot quite possess, and this is one source of narrative satisfaction. If we could *never* possess it, however, our excitation might become intolerable and turn into unpleasure; so we must know that the object will finally be restored to us. (quoted in Schnell 274)

*If we could* never *possess it … our excitation might become intolerable.*
    Schnell ultimately finds the distance she needs to mourn Claire's loss, as she puts it, "in other people's stories." She writes,

> The truth of it was, my compulsion to read had somewhat less to do with subject matter than it had to do with the simple fact of beautiful words on the page and the way they could draw me into the space that is the gap between the real and the expressed or imagined life. (277)

Proper mourning, Schnell realizes, requires space, but a certain kind of space, the kind of space created by linguistic and narrative representation. Proper mourning requires narrative.

The "wild country of time" is a place where things only ever go missing; planting our narrative flags in its inhospitable soil and claiming a piece of its ground as our own, though perhaps ultimately a futile gesture, is nonetheless what we must do to survive the pain of this life, to get to the "there" that must follow the "gone. (278)

Kathryn Schulz tells us that "we will lose everything we love in the end" but that "by definition, we do not live in the end: we live along the way." Everything we love will move from one space to another, will pass from this world to the next. But it is narrative, so fragile at times, that has the power to help us mourn. The telling. The learning how to tell.

"And so we repeat our stories, and we listen to others'," Susan Brison reminds us. Brison cites Eva Hoffman, who reminds us that

To a large extent, we're the keepers of each other's stories, and the shape of these stories has unfolded in part from our interwoven accounts. Human beings don't only search for meanings, they are themselves units of meaning; but we can mean something only within the fabric of larger significations. (quoted in Brison 58)

My siblings and I are the keepers of my mother's stories, but we keep them in ways we both can and cannot be aware of. One of the ways I keep my mother's stories is in my own need to tell stories, to hear stories, and to leave, everywhere I go, personally and professionally, a trail of stories proving that I exist, that I was here, that I made more than just an argument.

# 5 We Are All Telling It Slant

> And the story is the most dangerous thing there is. Because the way we talk about what happened *becomes* what happened.
>
> —Molly Brodak, *Bandit*

Emily Dickinson cautioned readers to "tell all the truth but tell it slant," and the advice to *tell it slant* is commonplace in creative nonfiction programs, courses, and how-to books; in fact, it comprises part or even all of the title of more than one of those how-to creative nonfiction books. To tell it slant suggests, of course, that there is a way to tell it straight, that a story is something that can be bent to one's will, that its actors, actions, plotlines, values, ideologies—all of these can be represented honestly, or *straight*, or they can be represented creatively, or *slant*. Telling a story the way my mother did all her life—via cautions like *Don't get pregnant before you get married* or *Marry a rich man*—was her way of telling her story slant, but we kids could not know this until, in her late seventies, her dementia insisted that she tell her story straight.

I have been telling the story of my abortion slant for decades now, first as an undergraduate student in my honors thesis ("Verbal Gymnastics: The Rhetoric of the Abortion Debate") and now as a teacher of rhetoric. In the years immediately following Michael breaking up with me, I told some friends the story straight, but since that time, as a teacher working to help students understand the concepts of ideology and stasis theory, I use the stark nature of the abortion debate in this country to help them understand the difference between pro-life ideology, whose primary claim is that the life of the unborn child is paramount, and pro-choice ideology, whose primary claim is that a woman should have the right to decide what to do with her own body. It never fails that I spend more time on the latter argument, that I make very clear where I stand on the issue, and I tell students this unapologetically. I am telling them my story slant. One day perhaps I will become strong enough (though this is problematic, as it suggests that right now I am weak) to share my story with them straight. The straight story being that, as

Valerie Tarico, writing in *Salon.com* in September 2015, suggests, "The prudence or wisdom of an abortion may be obvious at the time, but the power and the full meaning of that decision only begin to come into focus in the years and decades that follow." The very fact that I am *there*, that I am standing in front of *this* class of students talking to them about the abortion debate in this country—rather than home with a child or, given that that child would be grown by now, in a very different kind of career—suggests something about the full meaning of that decision I made in 1990. My hunch is that many women tell their abortion stories slant this way or they tell the abortion stories of their friends slant this way. My hunch, in other words, is that our academic and intellectual attachments reveal something about our stories.

This is not a difficult claim to make. Ask the scholar of cryptography about her childhood and you will learn that her very earliest diaries were written in cipher because she did not trust the people she lived with. Ask the scholar of masculinity studies about his parents and you will learn that his father struggled with expressions of toxic masculinity his entire life. The work we study is rarely accidental. We do not just stumble upon a subject and decide, willy-nilly, to study it. We are telling our stories slant.

But we in composition and writing studies are loath to acknowledge that we do so, largely because of our distrust of narrative; there is a reluctance to admit that we are attached to our work in ways that come before the intellectual. If it is personal, it is too simple, or so we believe.

I think we can fool some of the people some of the time. But life is more than argument. Life is story. And as Molly Brodak writes in her memoir *Bandit*, "the way we talk about what happened *becomes* what happened." If the way we talk about writing in composition and writing studies is as argument or as genre studies or as something to be assessed, that is what writing *becomes*. Writing is no longer a "guidance system that directs attention," providing "terms of *selection*—what to pay attention to—and following immediately is the need for *evaluation*, or what to think about what has been selected. Stories work as people's *selection/evaluation* system" (Frank, *Letting* 46).

I think sometimes even we forget that we are telling it slant, that the work we do began with us, with our *selves*. Twenty years ago, Richard E. Miller wrote, in his beautiful essay "The Nervous System," that

> Sustaining a self and sustaining a culture are ceaseless activities. Both projects are always under construction and always under repair, although this endless work may escape our notice until a moment of crisis makes the grinding of the machinery suddenly audible to us. To engage actively in the process of constructing a self is to replace a sense of destiny with the vision of an uncertain future. Similarly, to think of culture as not only present in a series of intellectual debates carried out in the academy but also as the varying registers of taste

and distaste physically experienced in the body is to take down the cordon separating the public and the private and to recognize that all intellectual projects are always, inevitably, also autobiographies. (285)

Miller's work is a large part of the exigency for my work in this book, for it is there that I first saw uttered straight, rather than slant, what he calls "the expression of a desire to be seen [that] elicits a response other than revulsion" (278). We all want to be seen. We all express these desires to be seen in any number of ways: by writing and delivering conference papers, by writing academic articles, by publishing academic books, by accepting award nominations, hell, by *teaching*. All of these expressions of the desire to be seen are *slant* expressions. Telling our stories, asking for our stories to be heard, are *straight* expressions of the desire to be seen. And perhaps it is for this reason that we in composition and writing studies turn away. For even Emily Dickinson told us to tell the truth but tell it slant, for "The Truth must dazzle gradually/ Or every man be blind—."

*

There is another way of thinking about a story as being straight—as something that must be *kept* straight—this, as opposed to something that we might forget. *Slant* in this case would be a metaphor for forgetting. Or, keeping a story straight is keeping all of its details in a row, memorized, unprocessed. Susan Brison writes of the requirement that she keep the story of her rape and attempted murder straight for the trial, for in the context of the judicial system, any differences between one telling and another would be cause for concern. "When the verdict was announced … I felt an instantaneous physical response: my body was shaking, wracked with sobs, although I didn't feel sad or elated," Brison writes.

> I didn't really feel anything but a sudden unclenching. I didn't have to keep the story straight. It didn't matter any longer if I got it right. I could let go of the details I'd kept alive in my mind, the narrative I'd remembered, rehearsed, and, finally, delivered to the court. (108)

After rehearsing for us all of the details she had been required to keep straight, Brison acknowledges that "Now I could, in a sense, forget what had happened to me. Now I could afford to think about it" (109). The implication here is clear: in order to think about what had happened to her, in order to process it, to reflect on it, Brison needed to stop re-hearsing it, stop repeating it. She needed to narrativize it for others. The story she told needed not to be kept straight but to wander, to become something that could live and breathe and grow as her understanding of it did.

Ma's stories were straight but came out slant. They never grew and breathed because they were never processed and never narrativized for others. Instead they fossilized. They remained stuck in homeostasis. In a recent essay in the *New Yorker*, Siddhartha Mukherjee marvels at the body's homeostasis, the constant work that must be accomplished behind the scenes, so to speak, to keep the body in stasis. Writing of the time before his father's death, Mukherjee writes that the things we never notice are not, therefore, worth not noticing:

> These conserving, self-correcting, decay-resisting forces that contend invisibly within us—in our bodies, our cities, our planetary ecosystem, even—are the opposite of nothing. The hospitals that work, the ambulances that lift patients smoothly off the ground: we neglect the small revolutions that maintain these functions, but when things fall apart we are suddenly alert to the chasms left behind. If we could measure homeostatic stamina—if we could somehow capture and quantify resilience—we might find a way to conserve things worth keeping before they failed, or, for that matter, learn to break things that we wanted broken. It is easy to notice the kind of activity that drives change; stasis, on the other hand, requires a more vigilant reckoning. (35)

*We might learn to break things that we wanted broken* if, say, we were better able to recognize the resilient quality of cultural narratives that persuade us that, say, a secret kept is best continued kept; a mistake made long ago is something to be ashamed of; the pain we carry with us cannot be shared with others lest they judge us; parents cannot be understood by their children. Children will judge their parents. We might learn to break these. I want to break them. Tell these stories.

Further, we might learn, if we notice the work that goes into maintaining the homeostasis of argument in composition and writing studies, to break the story that suggests that writing from one's personal experience is less valuable than collating material known to be in the public sphere. One way to break this story is to point to the sexist underpinnings of such beliefs, for whose stories but men's have been deemed to be worthy of recording for public consumption? Whose stories have been written down? Whose stories have been relegated to the private and the personal? Why do we, a field that prides itself for working always for social justice, continue to carry this prejudice?

\*

Joan Didion famously wrote that "it is easy to see the beginnings of things, and harder to see the ends." The exact opposite is true in stories of dementia, for it is difficult to pinpoint exactly where dementia begins, and it is easy as pie to see where it ends, for it always ends the same way.

It always ends with the body forgetting itself. It ends with the body mercifully forgetting how to breathe.

*

My biggest fear is losing my mind. It is not dying or losing Steve or losing either of my dogs but losing the things I value the most, and that is my mind. My cognitive capacity. My ability to make something, sometimes, of what seems like nothing. My ability to process complicated material, to take what initially seems like one thing and to realize, after much complex thought, that it is really another. My biggest fear is not turning into my mother—I realize that that is a common fear among middle-aged women. Rather, my biggest fear is turning into a hollowed-out, storyless version of myself. We are the stories we tell about ourselves. From the time I was small, the most valuable thing about me was my smarts. If I lose that, I've got nothing.

*

"We have all forgotten much more than we remember," writes Lynn Casteel Harper in her essay "On Vanishing." "The proliferation of vanishing, more and more, is what we have."

One of the things I realized as I wrote these essays is that the cautions about men are the ones I remembered the most. The one I had the hardest time remembering was the one she would say about how she wasn't going to watch our babies when we had them. She was not going to spend her days with our screaming kids.

Ma was the first person who taught me to be a critic—of men, mostly. She taught me to be critical of them, endlessly. They were no good. They were ugly. They were mostly stupid. "If he had a brain, he'd be dangerous," she would often say about my stepfather, Warren. "He's a horse's ass," she would say about this man or that. She taught me to be wary of them, to never trust them, but also to depend on them for material goods. She taught me that they were the only way I could survive. Marry a rich doctor, she said. Though she would never have called herself a feminist—a woman's libber—she instilled in me some crude feminist beliefs. Men were not, in so many ways, my better.

My mother did not read to me, but I wonder, if she had, what she would have chosen for me. In her essay "The Useful Dangers of Fairy Tales," Amber Sparks writes of the value of traditional fairy tales' warnings about the dangers of the world. In response to children's books written with empowered female lead characters, Sparks writes,

> I want us to stop pretending that if we say a thing is so, it must be so. We can write as many books as we want about heroine

princesses conquering the world—and I welcome them—but it doesn't stop women from being stalked, being doxed, from being harassed, silenced, raped, married off, targeted, kept fighting for our reproductive rights. It's one thing to help our daughters understand that they have it within themselves to be smart, to be tough, to take on the world on their own terms. It's another thing entirely to whitewash the very real difficulties they (and their mothers) almost certainly will face, regardless of how empowered they are. We are born into a certain world, and how we navigate that world is part spunk and part, frankly, wariness and warning.

Traditional fairy tales, Sparks points out, "warn rather than extol. They're useful, which is a much older kind of feminism." My mother, it seems to me, would have agreed with Sparks, who sees the value of fairy tales' cautions, writing that "part of the way I'd like to protect them, and to protect my daughter and her generation, too, is to draw the face of evil so they recognize it, then and not-so-long-ago."

The faces of evil for my mother, and so for us girls, were men who had the power to get us pregnant. But now, as I think about the warnings she wanted us to hear and the ones I did hear, I wonder if she put more emphasis on some rather than others. I wonder if what she wanted us to hear and what we heard were the same. I wonder, in other words, if she put more emphasis on being sure to have more than one child, but I pay less attention to that warning because I had no children. I wonder if she had been trying to tell a story about Pam, about her dying or about her saving Ma as a teenager.

I can never know.

*

Nineteen years after Michael broke up with me rather unceremoniously at the beginning of our junior year of college, we reconnected on Facebook. I should revise that sentence. I contacted *him* on Facebook because I wanted to share with him some writing I had been doing about that time in our lives. I wanted him to read my version of things, and it's clear to me now that what I was really doing was saying to him in no uncertain terms, "This is how it was for me." He read what I had written eagerly, and he even agreed to write his own impressions of Margie during that time for me. We wrote back and forth regularly, reminiscing about our first dates together, quizzing one another about who remembered which details, and it became clear as we did so that memory became a stand-in for devotion, even all these years later. But what we came to learn was that I remembered the big picture while Michael remembered the very fine details. I remembered *that* we made out in some park some-where on one of our first dates, while Michael remembered that it was

Buttery Brook park and we fogged up the windows and a police officer knocked on the window to check if we were "okay." Move along, he told us.

Though I've always thought about the abortion as my story to tell, it was Michael's too, and getting back in touch with him made me realize that he had been carrying that story with him, managing it, and it had been working on him in ways I could never have guessed. Michael told me that he had always regretted betraying my trust and telling his parents about the abortion. Here are his exact words:

> My father and I have always been so close that when he confronted me about it, I felt I owed him the truth. My parents have never brought it up again to me, and to this day I have always felt like I failed them … like always having that one thing hanging over my head from being the "perfect" son in their eyes. I even began to think I was being punished for our decision when my wife and I wanted to start a family. For over a year we couldn't get pregnant. Then when it finally happened she miscarried … then another miscarriage … and then a third. It was horrible, and I constantly thought about this being payback in some way. Still we kept on trying, and we were lucky enough to have two beautiful girls who have changed my life forever.

An abortion is a sin that must be punished. This is the narrative that dogs Michael in the years that follow our breakup and his young marriage. He is no longer the perfect son. His wife must suffer through three miscarriages before finally being able to carry a child to term because Michael and his seventeen-year-old girlfriend made the decision to terminate a pregnancy years before. In this kind of morality play, the scales must be balanced, and in Michael's way of understanding things, one abortion is equal to three miscarriages. One intentional termination is equal to three unintentional terminations.

I later asked Michael how many people he had shared the story of the abortion with, and his response is consistent with his understanding that *others* likely understand the decision to have an abortion as a difficult one, despite the fact that we did not find this to be the case. He writes,

> The story I have always told has an air of shame to it … not one necessarily of regret, but more of, I'm not proud of this but think it's important for you to know this about me type of thing. Even though there really was no question of what the decision was going to be for us, I have always told the story that it was a very difficult decision, I guess if nothing else to come across as not being heartless to those that may have different beliefs with the issue. The main story told was a complete chronological series of events that led to the abortion including going to counselors, court, etc.

Michael anticipated his audience's emotional response to a story in which he and his teenage girlfriend make a relatively quick decision to terminate a pregnancy, and he wards off any harsh judgments by intimating instead that it was a difficult decision. People who decide rather easily to have an abortion are to be judged just as easily, this narrative suggests. If you know yourself and you know your life and you know what you would be giving up by bringing that life into this world, you are to be judged. Instead, you should have agonized. Tell that story instead. Make it up if you have to. That's the narrative world we all want to live in.

Amy Shuman writes that "Sometimes when people tell their life stories, they tell more than one story. They tell what happened, and they tell what might have happened." This is exactly what Michael did, both when he told others about our difficult decision and when he told me the story of *telling the story* of our difficult decision. Imagine, for a minute, Amy, if our decision had been a difficult one. But it never, ever was. Shuman continues,

> Narratives are told from the middle of unfinished business; they negotiate the present as much or more than the past. Rather, the relationship between narratives and their possible trajectories is more complex and more a matter of mapping parable or allegory onto narrative or example onto experience than of opening up closings. Understanding the multiple trajectories and multiple footings narratives offer is one way to comprehend how narrative constrains or subverts cultural categories. (85)

Because Michael interpreted his wife's miscarriages in the context of my abortion, they took on an allegorical meaning they might not otherwise have had for him. Likewise, one could easily look at my situation today, learn that I had an abortion at the age of seventeen, and narrate a story in which my abortion becomes the *cause* of my not having any children. The abortion comes to carry so much weight in each of our lives, but only because we live in a culture that assigns it this much weight. I was never going to have children, and *that* is the one of the reasons for the abortion. But that is not a narrative that helps to make sense of other people's moral judgments.

Sarah Smarsh writes that "Belief and doubt are inevitably selfish things. But beyond our dubious ability to judge a story is something transcendent: our ability to receive it. Memoirists aren't making an argument. They're making an offering."

\*

I have been chasing narrative all my life. I've never outgrown the childish desire to have someone tell me a story. We seek, all our lives, the things we are deprived of when we are young. I was never told stories as a kid. Instead, they were withheld from me. Kept from me. Secreted away. I knew next to nothing about my father, who died when I was four. I knew next to nothing about my mother, who died when I was forty-one. Ma told us stories only in distress, at the end of her life, and by that point, we couldn't hear them. We didn't know what she was talking about.

I think because of this, I've been inexorably drawn to excellent, exuberant storytellers, and I have often confused the practice of storytelling with the expression of care.

I have always been an excellent receiver of stories. I pay careful attention, I laugh in all the right places, I ask all the right questions, I make the storyteller feel *listened to*. When we consider, then, the work of stories—what they do, how they direct our attention, how we get caught up in them, "with what effect, and to the exclusion of what other possible stories" (Frank 139)—we might also consider the work of the story*hearer*. For without the attention required to listen to a good story, a story cannot do its agentive work. A story cannot connect us to one another, teach us what to value, teach us how to see and how to ignore. If we aren't paying attention, we might just miss the detail that it was *babies* Ma was talking about all along, not just *the baby*.

*

I tried, years ago, to write some of these stories straight, without theorizing or processing them in the ways I've learned to do as an academic writer, but I quickly became bored. I wasn't learning anything. Just as my mother couldn't tell her story straight because it offered no protection, I couldn't tell these stories straight because doing so offered me so very little work to do. I wanted to *essay*; I wanted to put things next to one another and see what happened. But I couldn't do the other extreme, either. I cannot write only about story or about narrative in the abstract (is there even a way of doing such thing?) so that my own subjectivity does not infect or inflect upon what I write. And if I'm really being honest about what I'm figuring out in the process of doing this work, I'll say this: if we, as a field, continue to pretend that we do all the work we do for scholarly and intellectual reasons only, we will continue to expect others to carry our negative emotions for us. We will expect that others, those who are in creative writing or in the arts or in psychology, will work through why we're doing what we're doing, and we won't have to. We can continue to live with narratives that tell us that abortion causes miscarriages or that secrets are best kept or that children cannot help their parents or that students who turn their work in late are troublemakers or that stories are for those ill-equipped with theory. We can continue to live in morality plays that tell us that single mothers deserve to be poor, that rape victims somehow had it coming, and that angry dispositions cause cancer.

We can continue to do this. And we will continue to see more and more violence.

"Listen," writes Rebecca Solnit,

> You are not yourself, you are crowds of others, you are as leaky a vessel as was ever made, you have spent vast amounts of your life as someone else, as people who died long ago, as people who never lived, as strangers you never met. The usual *I* we are given has all the tidy containment of the kind of character the realist novel specializes in and none of the porousness of our every waking moment, the loose threads, the strange dreams, the forgettings and misrememberings, the portions of a life lived through others stories, the incoherence and inconsistency, the pantheon of dei ex machina and the companionability of ghosts. There are other ways of telling. (*Faraway* 248)

As a field, we have for so long wanted to not want to believe in the value of story. In order to become a field that values the work of story, we not only have to change our collective minds about story, we have to repudiate the version of ourselves that does not value the work of story. As Hilde Lindemann explains,

> Changing one's mind, especially about something that involves a moral commitment, is not simply a matter of choosing Y where you previously chose X. You also have to *repudiate* X (Nelson 2009). And that is a second-order desire, because repudiation is a matter of not wanting to want something anymore. If this desire moves you to act, you've exercised your second-order volition. (138)

This work would need to happen on the organizational level, on the programmatic level, and on the individual level. As a field, we would need to repudiate the version of ourselves that previously chose to devalue the work of story. Campus programs would have to repudiate earlier versions of themselves that did not value story, and individual people like you and me would have to acknowledge not just that we value the work of story, but that we want to value it and that we no longer want to be the people we once were: those who did not value the work of story. That is a tall order in a field that has for so long staked its identity in argument and academic writing.

"An argument is only an emergency of self-definition," writes Rachel Cusk in her personal essay, "Aftermath." Consider Solnit's thoughts on emergency:

If an emergency is an accelerated emergence, merge is the opposite condition, "to immerse or plunge (a person, esp. oneself) in a specified activity, way of life, environment, etc." or "to immerse or plunge in a liquid" or "to cause to be incorporated, absorbed, or amalgamated". (250)

A personal essay is an immersive undertaking characterized by calm, care, methodical consideration of this and that, of the *how* and the *why*, the *how not* and the *why not*. A personal essay is not some two-sided beast emergency but rather a complex interweaving of narrative, analysis, and commentary. It requires that we repudiate none of the things on which we've staked our identities through the decades.

*

At Ma's funeral, one of the stories Susie wanted to tell was about the time when, as a kid, Susie pointed out an ugly dog and Ma said, "No. There are no ugly dogs. All animals are beautiful." Though she told me again and again to be wary of men and to have children so they could care for me when I got old, she didn't tell me so much as show me how important it was to appreciate the kind of love that only animals can give. She loved her cats with a ferocity that I'm sure all of us kids envied at different points in our lives. Because cats loved her back without ambivalence. They snuggled her on cool nights, they responded gratefully when she fed them, and they listened to her and rarely talked back. Watching a wildlife show on television, she'd call us into the room so she could share with us the beauty of a mountain lion or a grizzly bear. "Amy, c'mere! Look look look look look lookit. Lookit the kangaroo!" When I adopted my first dog in my late twenties after I broke up with my boyfriend Al, I'd bring Annabelle to visit when I'd come home from school in Syracuse. Though Annabelle stole more than just a hot dog bun from her when she wasn't looking, Ma loved her, and I think she understood how much I loved that dog.

The enormity of her love for animals made it that much harder for her to acknowledge her grief when they died. I don't remember her crying for Mindy or Mr. Cat or Sandy, and when I called to tell her that we'd had to put Annabelle down, she told me not to cry. I wonder now if, on some level, she knew she couldn't cry for those sweet kitties because if she started she might never stop. As she aged, though, she softened a bit and permitted herself to voice grief over her Baxter boy. One of the things age—and eventually dementia—did was to break down some of her walls.

In her memoir, *New Life, No Instructions*, Gail Caldwell writes,

The ... thing I know ... is that we survive grief merely and surely by outlasting it—the ongoing fact of the narrative eclipses the heart-break within, a deal that seems to be the price we pay for getting to hold on to our beloved dead.

When I wonder how Ma survived so much grief in her life, I realize that she simply outlasted it. So much pain, so much sorrow, so much unacknowledged grief. She just kept on going. This was no small feat.

The two people who I will always think about as *the babies* have grown up to be adults somewhere in this world. They would be in their mid- to late-sixties by now, with lives full of stories of their own, stories that began on those same days when my mother's story—and so all of my siblings' stories and my own—shifted so dramatically. Their stories, like all of ours, are best told slant.

"The point of a story," Carolyn Kay Steedman writes, "is to present itself momentarily as complete, so that it can be said: it does for now, it will do; it is an account that will last for a while."

It will change. It must. A story is a living creature; it lives, breathes, and grows.

# Epilogue

We Robillards are a loud people. Though Ma wasn't born a Robillard, she, too, was loud. Her sneezes could wake the dead, and her laugh, if you weren't prepared for it, could scare the shit out of you. My dad had a wicked laugh, too, and his laugh served as the laugh track for the Fun House at Mountain Park in Holyoke, Massachusetts, a now-defunct amusement park we'd go to as kids. I never knew this tiny detail until I was an adult. I wish I had known it as a kid. My dad's laugh *defined* the Fun House.

*

In her essay, "The Essayist Is Sorry for Your Loss," Sara Levine writes,

> Another thing that makes the essay seem like a mess is its refusal to decide the things it feels like it cannot decide. The essay is willing to harbor contradictions. Like a hotel for disagreements, like a pillow on which discrepancy can rest her rumpled head. The article likes contradictions too but it starts with them and tries to resolve them; or it starts with something that doesn't look like a contradiction at all, and methodically shows it to be one. Either way contradictions are cunningly displayed in such a way that the contradiction appears to be located outside—outside in a text, outside in the culture, more importantly, outside of the author. (284)

*

Composition and writing studies has a vexed relationship with narrative, especially with narratives that claim to be personal. In this way, the field is very much like my mother.

Arthur Frank draws on the work of Pierre Bayard to describe what he calls one's narrative habitus. Each of us has an inner story, which, Frank explains, "predisposes which future stories a person will seek out, feel comfortable with, be able to learn from, and remember." Frank continues,

According to the psychoanalytic aspect of Bayard's argument, people spend their lives seeking a story that can match the inner story. This search will never end, because each actually encountered story will necessarily be an imperfect representation of the inner story, or chimerical imagination of a story. Seeking stories becomes a process of displacement—each next story displacing the imperfect one before, seeking what can never be found. The Holy Grail—the mythic cup that caught Christ's blood and is the object of quests by King Arthur's knights in medieval romances—symbolizes the perfect inner story. Grail stories can be read reflexively as stories about the quest for the ideal story, which will effect all final healing and reconciliation. Or, the story that, once told, will quench desire for any other stories. The attraction of Grail stories is tied to the hope that all this questing—or displacement in psychoanalytic terms— might someday end; that there is a telos, a finish line, a homecoming after which no travel is necessary. Psychic reality is closer to the end of Homer's *Odyssey*; having finally returned home, Odysseus is sent off on another journey, and only the reader's need for an ending suggests that this next journey will be any shorter than the one from which he has just returned. (57)

I think of the inner story as sort of what people who are addicted to heroin describe themselves trying to do after that first high: always trying to recreate it, never able to quite get there. What is my Grail story? What are the Grail stories for each of my siblings? What are the stories that, once we find them, effect all final healing and reconciliation? What are the stories we need to hear?

For a long time, I was upset that I wasn't the one my mother was searching for. When she had that first stroke and in a panic asked Guy where the baby was, she meant me, certainly. Except, with Guy asking her right then and there if she meant me, she said no. And with the years passing and our learning the truth about the babies she was really searching for, she said no again. I wasn't the one she was searching for. Though I would always be her baby, I wasn't *the baby*. I wasn't the one would could heal her in the way I imagine I healed her after my father died.

But that's not my Grail story. I figured out my Grail story by reading, as I've figured out so many other things in this life.

When I was a kid I wanted desperately to be Laura Ingalls. I watched *Little House on the Prairie* whenever I could, though Guy and I fought over the TV on Monday nights because he wanted to watch *That's Incredible!* I wanted a father who called me Half-Pint. I wanted cute buck teeth and perfect braids with a perfectly straight line down the middle of my scalp. I wanted bonnets and flowered dresses, and on Sundays, I wanted my mother to tie my braids into big teardrops on either side of my head, finished with a bow that matched the fabric of my Sunday finest. I wanted

Pa to take me in to town whenever he went. I wanted to wave to the other families as they waved at us. I wanted so badly to feel loved.

But now I realize that what I wanted even more than to feel loved was to feel protected. My Grail story is a story of protection. I figured this out by reading Tara Westover's memoir, *Educated*, in the spring of 2018. *Educated* is billed by most reviewers as the story of a young girl who educates herself enough to escape her survivalist family and go on to earn a PhD. But for me it's a memoir about sibling abuse, about the scars that never heal, about the need for protection from our own family members, and there's a moment in the book when Tara's mother acknowledges that, yes, she knew that Shawn had been beating Tara. *"You were my child. I should have protected you."* When I read those words, I became Tara because I needed to become her, and for just a moment, Tara's mother became my mother, and she acknowledged that she had not been the mother to me that she should have been. She acknowledged that she should have protected me from my older sister Margie. And it was in that moment that I realized that all of the stories I've ever been drawn to, the ones that pull me in—the ones that suck me in with a force I cannot describe—are ones in which the vulnerable are protected by characters from whom the vulnerable weren't necessarily expecting that protection. They had given up. But somehow that protection is offered and some small degree of healing is begun. This is the story I've been seeking all my life.

My desire for protection stories will never be quenched, in all likelihood. But perhaps, I'll respond to them differently now that I know what they represent to me—the unattainable, the absence in the middle of me.

What is the Grail story for our field? What is the story we seek again and again, never feeling fully satisfied? Is it a story about the relationship between the academic and the personal? Is it a story about our role in the academy? Is it a story about our own significance? Do we, once we get too close to it, recoil, only to tell a different, face-saving story? I do not profess to know, but I suspect that there is some element of fear that keeps us from seeking the many different kinds of stories our colleagues have to tell.

*

The few times I can remember an adult asking me what I wanted to be when I grew up, I can remember responding that I wanted to be either a fireman (masculine pronoun) or Little Red Riding Hood. I clearly had a thing for running into, not away from, danger. Interestingly, Charles Perrault's version of Little Red Riding Hood, in which the little girl is eaten by the wolf, cautions all little girls to "stay on guard against all sorts of men."

My mother's cautionary tales, taken together, were the remnants of a screen story that she could never tell us because to do so would be to risk too much shame. To do so would be to acknowledge that *she* was the cautionary tale.

Well, I've grown up.
I'm neither a fireman nor Little Red Riding Hood.
And I've heeded none of my mother's cautions.
I haven't stayed away from men.
Sometimes I went behind the bushes with them.
I *did* get pregnant before I got married.
I *didn't* marry a rich man.
I *didn't* have more than one child. In fact, I have had no children at all.
I *haven't* been very careful about what I've wished for.

My mother was not unlike so many other mothers who don't want to see their own children make the same mistakes they themselves made when they were young. What made her different, I think, was that she was rarely kind about this desire—her edicts were issued without empathy or compassion—and that behind her edicts was a story she would never be able to tell.

Stories are not unequivocally empowering. The ones that do not change, the ones that fossilize because they are not told—those can kill a person. The ones that are never reinterpreted, the ones that are trotted out again and again to serve a purpose that has nothing to do with their audience and everything to do with their narrator—those are not stories. They're defense mechanisms. They're narcissistic supports. They're weapons.

I think I'm done chasing certain kinds of narratives. I'm done chasing the kind that stand still, the kind that have me running in place. I've run past those now. I want to see what lies beyond them. I want, instead, to essay.

My interest in the personal essay makes me wary of certainty. But that's not entirely true. Nothing is entirely true. I am interested in some kinds of certainty: the kind that tells me that my body is physically safe, the kind that tells me I'm emotionally safe. The kind of certainty, in other words, that those who have been abused cannot take for granted, the kind that allows me to say that I cherish the uncertainty of the personal essay. At its most basic, abuse is a violation of trust. Trust depends on certainty. The writing process depends upon trusting oneself to venture into unknown places. For all of our talk in composition and writing studies about process, we have not examined the extent to which engaging in writing processes depends upon trusting oneself and the extent to which trusting oneself depends upon safety.

*

Once the narratives on which I shaped an identity collapsed right as I was approaching forty years old, I had to stitch together new ones. I'm still doing that work. I know now that my mother was the mother she was not only because she lost her husband and daughter within five months of each other, but because, too, she lost two newborn babies when she was so very young, and those losses imprinted on her psyche in ways she was never able to work through. She was not able to offer the very thing I needed as I was growing up, and because of that, I seek, everywhere I go, an understanding of what it means to care and to protect. I am building a narrative of myself as a person who cares and protects in safe ways—not in ways that give too much of myself, for that is the way I cared for too long. I gave too much of myself away, leaving nothing for me because I didn't believe I deserved anything. I would be loved if I gave and gave and gave. I would be loved if I took on other people's problems as my own, never claiming to have problems of my own that needed attending to. I would be loved if I effaced myself.

My mother had very little to give by the time she had me. She did what she could, and she gave me a great deal. I believed I had very little to give when I started out in this life, when I started out in this profession. I gave and gave and gave and now, as I realize how much I actually do have to give, I give less. I talk with graduate students, women especially, all the time how to say no. I am learning to protect myself, though I'd much rather have someone else do it for me. But it's too late for that. I'm too old for that.

I find myself in other people's stories of protection, learning how they accept it, learning how they practice it, trying it on for myself. I practice it for myself, getting better week by week, month by month, year by year, until, one day, maybe, I will have protected myself well enough that I have found my holy Grail. I will have achieved some form of healing and reconciliation, seeking in other people's stories not hope but recognition.

# Works Cited

Anderst, Leah. "Feeling With Real Others: Narrative Empathy in the Autobiographies of Doris Lessing and Alison Bechdel." *Narrative* 23.3 (October 2015): 271–290.

Bachelard, Gaston. *Water and Dreams*. Dallas: Dallas Institute for Humanities and Culture, 1999.

Bizzell, Patricia. "Rationality as Rhetorical Strategy at the Barcelona Disputation, 1263: A Cautionary Tale." *College Composition and Communication* 58.1 (2006): 12–29.

Brison, Susan J. *Aftermath: Violence and the Remaking of a Self*. Princeton: Princeton UP, 2002.

Brodak, Molly. *Bandit: A Daughter's Memoir*. New York: Black Cat, 2016.

Brooks, Melanie. *Writing Hard Stories: Celebrated Memoirists Who Shaped Art from Trauma*. Boston: Beacon Press, 2017.

Butler, Judith. *Frames of War*. New York: Verso, 2010.

———. *Precarious Life: The Powers of Mourning and Violence*. New York: Verso, 2006.

Caldwell, Gail. *New Life, No Instructions*. New York: Random House, 2015.

Cobb, Sara. *Speaking of Violence: The Politics and Poetics of Narrative in Conflict Resolution*. New York: Oxford UP, 2013.

———. "Stabilizing Violence: Structural Complexity and Moral Transparency in Penalty Phase Narratives." *Narrative Inquiry* 20.2 (2010): 296–324.

Condon, William. "The Future of Portfolio-Based Writing Assessment: A Cautionary Tale." *Writing Assessment in the 21st Century: Essays in Honor of Edward M. White*. Norbert Elliot and Les Perelman, Eds. New York: Hampton Press, 2012.

Cusk, Rachel. "Aftermath." *Granta Magazine*. 19 May 2011.

Daum, Meghan. *The Unspeakable*. New York: Picador, 2015.

Didion, Joan. "Goodbye to All That." *Slouching Towards Bethlehem*. New York: Farrar, Straus, and Giroux, 1961.

Diller, Christopher, and Scott F. Oates. "Infusing Disciplinary Rhetoric into Liberal Education: A Cautionary Tale." *Rhetoric Review* 21.1 (2002): 53–60.

Diski, Jenny. "A Diagnosis." *London Review of Books*. September 2014.

Edginton, Anthony. "The Road to Mainstreaming: One Program's Successful but Cautionary Tale." *Discord and Direction: The Postmodern Writing Program Administrator*. Sharon James McGee, Ed. Logan: Utah State UP, 2005.

Fessler, Ann. *The Girls Who Went Away*. New York: Penguin, 2006.

Frank, Arthur W. *Letting Stories Breathe: A Socio-narratology.* Chicago: U of Chicago P, 2010.

———. "Tricksters and Truth Tellers: Narrating Illness in an Age of Authenticity and Appropriation." *Literature and Medicine* 28.2 (2009): 185–199.

———. "Writing Oneself Back In: Narratives of Care, Grief, and Loss." *Literature and Medicine* 35.1 (2017): 229–235.

Getty, Amy. "The Short and Sputtering Life of a Small Community College Writing Center: A Cautionary Tale." *Writing Lab Newsletter* 27.9 (2003): 10–12.

Graham, Margaret Baker, Elizabeth Birmingham, and Mark Zachry. "Reinventing First-Year Composition at the First Land-Grant University: A Cautionary Tale." *Writing Program Administration* 21.1 (1997): 19–30.

Griffin, Susan. *A Chorus of Stones.* New York: Anchor, 1993.

Hainey, Michael. *After Visiting Friends: A Son's Story.* New York: Scribner, 2013.

Harper, Lynn Casteel. "On Vanishing." *Catapult.* 7 April 2016.

Kahn, Seth. "(Re)politicizing the Writing Process: An Exhortation and a Cautionary Tale." *Activism and Rhetoric: Theories and Contexts for Political Engagement.* Seth Kahn and JongHwa Lee, Eds. New York: Routledge, 2011.

Keen, Suzanne. *Empathy and the Novel.* New York: Oxford UP, 2007.

King, Heather. "Of All the Mothers in the World." *The Sun.* August 2012.

Krause, Steven D. "When Blogging Goes Bad: A Cautionary Tale about Blogs, Emailing Lists, Discussion, and Interaction." *Kairos* 9.1 (2004).

Levine, Sara. "The Essayist Is Sorry for Your Loss." *Touchstone Anthology of Contemporary Creative Nonfiction.* Lex Williford and Michael Martone, Eds. New York: Simon & Shuster, 2007.

Lindemann, Hilde. *Holding and Letting Go: The Social Practice of Personal Identities.* New York: Oxford UP, 2014.

Marrett, Emily Garrigues. "When Bad Things Happen to Bad People: Using Disposition Theory to Explore the Effects of Cautionary Tales." *Journal of Health Communication* 20 (2015): 266–274.

Miller, Richard E. "The Nervous System." *College English* 58.3 (1996): 265–286.

Mukherjee, Siddhartha. "Bodies at Rest and in Motion." *The New Yorker.* 8 January 2018: 28–35.

Patchett, Ann. "Love Sustained." *Harper's Magazine.* November 2006.

Russell, Kent. "We Are Entering the Age of Alzheimer's." *New Republic.* 2 September 2014.

Schnell, Lisa. "Learning How to Tell." *Literature and Medicine* 23.2 (2004): 265–279.

Schulz, Kathryn. "When Things Go Missing." *The New Yorker.* 13 & 20 February 2017.

Sedgwick, Eve Kosofsky, and Adam Frank, Eds. *Shame and Its Sisters: A Silvan Tomkins Reader.* Durham: Duke UP, 1995.

Shuman, Amy. *Other People's Stories: Entitlement Claims and the Critique of Empathy.* Urbana: U of Illinois P, 2005.

Smarsh, Sarah. "Believe It." *Creative Nonfiction.* Spring 2015.

Solnit, Rebecca. *The Faraway Nearby.* New York: Viking, 2013.

———. "A Short History of Silence." *The Mother of All Questions*. Chicago: Haymarket Books, 2017.

Sparks, Amber. "The Useful Dangers of Fairy Tales." *LitHub.com*. 11 August 2017.

Specter, Michael. "Partial Recall." *The New Yorker*. 19 May 2014.

Steedman, Carolyn. *Landscape for a Good Woman*. New Brunswick: Rutgers UP, 1987.

Tarico, Valerie. "4 Ways to Change the Conversation about Abortion: Start with What Comes After." *Salon.com*. 3 September 2015.

Van Hartesveldt, Fred R. "The Undergraduate Research Paper and Electronic Sources: A Cautionary Tale." *Teaching History* 23.2 (1998): 51–59.

Watkins, Claire Vaye. "On Pandering." *Tin House*. 23 November 2015.

Westover, Tara. *Educated: A Memoir*. New York: Random House, 2018.

Wiman, Christian. "The Limit." *The Threepenny Review*. Fall 2001.

Yuknavitch, Lidia. "Woven." *Guernica*. 3 August 2015.

Zipes, Jack, Ed. *The Oxford Encyclopedia of Children's Literature*. Oxford: Oxford UP, 2006.

# Index

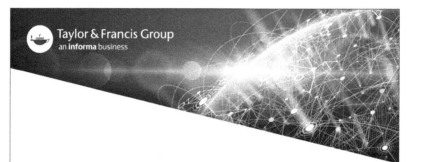

For Product Safety Concerns and Information please contact our EU
representative  GPSR@taylorandfrancis.com
Taylor & Francis Verlag GmbH, Kaufingerstraße 24, 80331 München, Germany

www.ingramcontent.com/pod-product-compliance
Ingram Content Group UK Ltd.
Pitfield, Milton Keynes, MK11 3LW, UK
UKHW021436080625
459435UK00011B/280